Born in Glasgow, Scotland, in 1943, Iain Winton migrated to Australia with his parents and siblings, in 1959, as a teenager. Iain spent the majority of his working life in local government, mainly in the fields of recreation, leisure, public relations, special events and promotions. His last major involvement before retiring was as the Olympic Coordinator for the city of Blacktown, responsible for Olympic softball and baseball competitions of the Sydney Olympics. Since retiring in 2001, he has pursued his interests of travel, golf, reading, writing and gardening and in 2009 became part of a musical group called, 'The Celtic Connection', which does concerts in the aged homes in the Sutherland Shire. Iain has long interest in poetry and had a number of poems published in magazines and books. In 2008, he self-published a book of poetry titled, *Iain with two 'I's*. His concern that Aussie kids didn't have much in the way of Australian Christmas stories was the impetus to write, *Wally the Hairy Nosed Wombat: An Australian Christmas Story*. This was his first children's story. Both books were well received. His second book of poetry called *My Cronulla* came out in 2019. Iain has lived in the Sutherland Shire with his wife of over forty years; he has two married daughters and five grand children.

In the memory of Mum and Dad who gave me such a lucky childhood; and to my father, David Winton, who I never got to know.

My father, David Winton in the uniform of the Gordon Highlanders

Iain Winton

The Last of the Lucky Childhoods

Growing Up in Glasgow in the '40s/'50s

Austin Macauley Publishers™

LONDON * CAMBRIDGE * NEW YORK * SHARJAH

A CIP catalogue record for this title is available from the British Library.

ISBN 9781528981477 (Paperback)
ISBN 9781528981484 (ePub e-book)

www.austinmacauley.com

First Published 2022
Austin Macauley Publishers Ltd®
1 Canada Square
Canary Wharf
London
E14 5AA

Table of Contents

1943–45 A War Baby   10

1948–51 Early Days   14

1950s – Street Games, Chittering Bites, Television and Specs   23

Christmas Was for Kids!!!   44

High School – Long Pants, Baggy Knees and The Strap   64

Scouting for Boys and Girls!   76

Holidays Were Happy Days!   86

Porridge, Mince and Tatties, Cod Liver Oil and Sugarolly Water!   96

1957–59 Teenage Years and New Horizons   101

Addendum to 'The Last of The Lucky Childhoods' (Poetry)   129

"…And Glasgow gave me more than it ever took away… And prepared me for life on the road…"

From the song *Glasgow* written and sung by
Billy Connolly

robiain1@bigond.com

1943–45 A War Baby

My name is Iain Macdonald Winton and I was born on 5th of January '43. It was towards the end of the war years and my mother gave birth to me at my maternal grandparent's home. My middle name came from my grandmother who was a Macdonald from the Isle of Skye.

My father, like his father, was a Gordon Highlander. He died of a blood clot on 14 February (St. Valentine's Day) on his way to re-join his regiment six weeks after I was born. He only saw me twice before he died, thus I have no recollection of him apart from photographs. His wedding ring and a small silver cup, which he won for athletics, are my only mementoes of him. His name is inscribed in the honour roll of the Gordon Highlander's regiment that rests in the war museum in Edinburgh Castle.

In March of '43, my mother had me christened at Jordenvale Church in Partick. I was the only one in the family to be christened due in part to the fact that my father's people were religious…this couldn't be said of the man who was to become my dad in a few years, for while he was a pacifist in his outlook, religion was not his suite.

Mum received a widow's pension from my father's regiment and for my first two years, my mother and I shared a bedroom at my grandparent's home with her twin sister and her son, Leslie, my elder cousin by three months.

Leslie's Dad was a regimental sergeant major serving in Italy. So Leslie and I grew up in a woman-dominated world, like many youngsters during World War II.

While the war was still being fought, Glasgow, as a major industrial city, was heavily targeted by the Germans. I was too young to have any recollections of those years, however, some stories that were told to me of these times still remains with me.

One such story was of our dog, a red setter named 'Rusty'. It seemed that each time Mum and my aunt Ruby (Leslie's Mum) took us boys out in our prams from a walk, Rusty would tag along. Rusty was our early warning signal, as before the air raid sirens would sound, he would alert us with a 'bark' and turn and race for home. Rusty died later in '43 and was sadly missed by all.

Thus, the first few years of my childhood passed mainly uneventfully, despite the war, though we had a near miss when a bomb exploded in the vicinity of our home blowing out the windows of the houses in the area.

I still carry two scars from those early days, however, they were nothing to do with the war. The first I got when I was only six months old, I fell off my mother's knee while being bottle fed (bottles in those days were made of glass) and cut my head on the broken bottle, the scar on my forehead there for all to see.

My second battle scar was when as a four-year-old, I rode my trike (tricycle) down the steep hill of Harefield Drive (the street I lived in), failed to take the corner at the bottom of the hill and went over the handlebars cutting my legs and hands on the gravel – my left hand still has some gravel embedded in it!

Another incident from which I survived unscathed, happened in London in '46 when Mum and I were out with my uncle Everly (Mum's older sister's husband) on his motorbike and sidecar; his handlebars jammed going round a corner and the bike went straight into a brick wall. Mum pushed me inside the hood of the sidecar and I was unhurt, but she sustained an ankle injury, which was to trouble her for the rest of her life.

Uncle Everly was a fire chief on London's Thames fireboats and I recall him taking me for a ride on his fireboat with its water cannons spraying plumes high in the air and its siren going full blast, which at my young age I found very exciting. My uncle in later years was to become the master-at-arms on the P&O's Oriana.

During this period, Mum was being steadily courted by my father's close friend, David Waddell (Uncle Dave to me). During the war, because he had declared himself a pacifist and was against taking up arms against his fellow man, he served in the 5th Company Carlisle (non-combatant company), mainly as a truck driver. I would receive postcards from him from all over the Low Countries telling me about his work and asking that I keep taking care of my mum.

Towards the end of '45, Uncle Dave went AWOL and visited Mum and me at Rothsay (where we spent some time during the years of '45 and '46). Unfortunately, he was caught by the military police and spent a few days in jail!

Following the end of the war, Uncle Dave continued his work in the Low Countries through the organisation known as the Quakers; he left this group on marrying Mum in '46.

In '46 when Mum remarried, Uncle Dave became my dad and I got the nickname 'Mac' which is still with me today, but only used by Dad, my middle daughter, Michelle, and a close friend, Father Foley. Dad gave me the name 'Mac' as my middle name was Macdonald; my grandmother from my father's side being a Macdonald from the Isle of Skye.

My 'new' Dad had been my father's close friend and had been best man at his wedding to my mother. Although Dad's name was Waddell, he kept my name Winton in memory of my father, and because I was the only remaining male in the Winton lineage – this was all to no avail as when I married I had three daughters!

My first name, Iain, was spelt the Gaelic way, meaning John. I was named after my father's brother, Uncle John Winton – also known as Jack…confusing isn't it? Uncle Jack was killed in Canada when he was training as a pilot for the royal air force, so I never got to know him.

My new dad and mum spent their honeymoon in Holland, where Dad had worked as a Quaker (Friends Relief Service) and they stayed with many of Dad's friends that he had made through this organisation. By all accounts they had a wonderful honeymoon, with Dad having to sell his wedding shoes to get back to Britain…and my brother, Alastair, being born in July '47.

After the war, housing in Glasgow was a problem; with too many families and too few houses, so most families lived under the same roof in an extended family atmosphere. We stayed with my maternal grandparents along with Aunt Ruby and Leslie. Not many people owned or bought their own houses in Glasgow and the major homeowner was the Glasgow Corporation Council which rented houses to the people.

Dad upon finding the situation a bit 'cramped' found lodgings with a friend of the family (whom I called Papa Noble…no wonder I was confused in my early years with four lots of grandparents!). We lived there till late '47 when Dad took up the offer of a position in the diploma course in youth services at Durham University, Newcastle upon Tyne. Dad found our lodgings in a boarding house at the seaside suburb of Whitley Bay and it was there that I attended my first school.

We lived there for two years while Dad completed his diploma. Again, I can recall little of this period apart from my contacting measles and whooping cough – common illnesses for children in that era.

My one vivid memory is that of being 'caught' by an incoming tide at Whitley Bay while crab hunting and having to be rescued with the sea waters up around my waist! The tides in this part of the country rise and fall at an exceptionally fast rate, and if you don't keep your eyes on the incoming tide you can get cut off from the sea wall, which was exactly what befell me.

In August of '48, Dad was offered the position of warden at Househillwood and Pollok Community Centre and we returned to Glasgow…

Over the next four years, the Waddell clan grew and I not only had a young brother but two sisters as well (Lana, born in '49 and Fiona, born in '51). That I had a different surname didn't seem to register with anyone nor did I question it till much later in life.

Mum and Dad treated us all the same and their love and affection was a major factor in my feelings that I grew up having a very lucky childhood.

1948–51 Early Days

With Dad finishing his studies at Durham University in Easter of '48, we returned once more to Glasgow staying again with Grandma Marshall (Mum's mother) at Harefield Drive, Scotstoun.

By this time, Mum's twin sister, Aunt Ruby, had moved with her husband and Leslie to their own home in Westerton, just outside of Glasgow, so Mum's older brother (Uncle Johnny) with his wife and baby son moved in to Harefield Drive, so we still had three families under one roof! My grandfather (Mum's father) passed away in this year; I don't remember much about him as I was too young, just that he was an elderly gentleman (he died at age 66) who always wore a suit with a waistcoat and a collar and tie.

I do, however, remember my Uncle Johnny, he was a tall thin man, he'd be called 'sprauchlie' in the Scots dialect; he always seemed to be smiling and walked, or rather strolled along with the kind of swaying gait of a sailor. He worked in the Albion workshops on the Clyde which made heavy vehicles such as lorries and buses. The Albion workshops were just about ten minutes' walk from our house, so Uncle Johnny used to walk to and from work daily. I can remember him strolling up Harefield Drive at the end of the day with a big smile on his face and he'd always greet the family with some words of humour. I don't remember him ever being upset or angry and I always got on pretty well with him.

His wife, Aunt Agnes, was another kettle of fish; she never seemed a happy person to me and was prone to complaining and comparing me to her son, Jim. Jim never seemed to do any wrong unlike me who was earning the label of the 'black sheep' of the family even at this early stage.

Dad became the warden of the Househillwood and Pollok Community Centre which was situated in the south-east of Glasgow, on the other side of the Clyde from where we lived. The Glasgow Corporation was one of the first local government areas to become involved in the concept of community work, and this was the role Dad carried out as warden.

I attended Scotstoun Primary School, which was about two miles from our house. As a wee boy, the walk home from school was somewhat daunting, especially in wintertime when it would be already dark with snow and frost on the ground. I was always glad when my 'granny' would come to pick me up…however, once home, it was out with my pals and sledging or sliding down the steep hill of our street! Cars were of little problem in those days and the streets were our playground.

The best place for making slides was on the footpaths, and this led to confrontation between the kids of the street and the adults – the slides made the pavements very unsafe, especially for the elderly and there would be a constant 'battle' between us kids making slides and the adults throwing salt on them (the salt making the ice melt).

My time at Scotstoun Primary School doesn't hold many memories for me apart from the ritual of wintertime when we'd go to school wrapped up in overcoats, scarfs and gloves and with our 'wellies' wet from the snow or slush. It was always a race to get a desk near the wall heaters so you could hang your wet clothes (including socks) on them and watch the steam rise as they dried out…if you were lucky enough they'd be dry before you had to go home.

Mind you, sometimes the smell of drying socks and 'wellies' was almost unbearable and the girls in the class would complain loudly to the teacher and you would dread the command of: "Winton! Put your socks and wellingtons back on at once – are you trying to gas us?" (this 'ritual' continued into high school until one graduated into 'proper' shoes in winter.)

I still have vivid recollections of my days at Harefield Drive, especially around the dinner table at night. Somehow, I just couldn't come at vegetables, especially brussels sprouts, cabbage and carrots. As these were part of the staple diet in those days, I had my problems!

My granny was somewhat understanding of my predicament and she would strain all the vegetables out of the 'scotch broth', so I'd only be left with the bree (she would also serve my dinner without vegetables)…This worked O.K. as long as Dad was not home from work!

However, if he was home it was a different matter. Dad had seen how the children of Europe had suffered from lack of food during and after the war and he was determined that none of his children would 'turn their noses up' at good food so I would have 'my' vegetables dumped back on my plate and be made eat them!!!

Sometimes I'd sit at the table for hours trying to stare down the vegetables, but to no avail. Often I'd await the chance (when Dad wasn't looking) and stuff the vegetables into my pockets then flush them down the toilet at the first chance I got; sometimes I'd stuff my cheeks with them, just like a pack rat and again dispose of them down the kitchen sink or the toilet. To this day I still have problems with 'veggies'.

Late in '48, I came down with scarlet fever (not enough vegetables?) and spent ten weeks in the hospital, worst of all over Christmas! I was sure that Santa would never find me but was most surprised and pleased when on Christmas morning there were presents all around my hospital bed. This latest childhood illness left me with a murmur at my heart. I had a recurrence of scarlet fever eighteen months later, however, the 'new' wonder drug penicillin was then available and I made a quick recovery.

When Mum came to take me home, we were just outside the hospital when three vampire jets screamed overhead. This was the first time I saw jet planes and one of our neighbours commented to us that these were the way wars of the future would be waged…considering that at that time, most deliveries in Glasgow to households were made by horse-and-cart and motor cars were still a rarity, it was a bold prediction.

There was a regular group of merchants that worked our streets in the '40s and '50s, each with his own horse-and-cart; they included the milkman, coalman, greengrocer and the kid's favourite, the 'rag-and-bone man'.

The rag-and-bone man would walk the streets calling out "rags and bones! Any old rags or bones!" This would make us kids rushing to our houses to see if we had any old clothing which we could exchange for a balloon on a stick or a white clay bubble pipe, or if you were really lucky and had lots of rags you would get a goldfish in a glass jar!

Try as I might, I could never get enough rags for a goldfish (people in the days after the war were very frugal and 'hand-me-downs' were of more worth than balloons or goldfish). However, I was determined to have a goldfish. So one day when the rag-and-bone man came around, I grabbed Dad's old suit (I'd heard him say it was old) and gave it to the rag-and-bone man and got my goldfish…Mum had to chase him down the street to get Dad's suit back…needless to say, I didn't get to keep my goldfish!

The only clothing I didn't have as 'hand-me-downs' were shoes. As I was the oldest of the family, my shoes were always new (perhaps it helped that both Mum and Dad had worked in the shoe department of one of Glasgow's large stores in their single days). Mind you, they made up in the frugality by always buying shoes one or two sizes too big and stuffing the toes with paper!

The horses and ponies belonging to these merchants were well trained and they would ply the streets unaided, stopping at the appropriate places for their masters to make deliveries. These animals also served the community in another way, as when they would do their droppings, neighbours would rush out with a spade and hessian bag to scoop up this manure for their gardens…nothing was wasted in those days!

Most families had vegetable gardens where they grew potatoes, cabbages, turnips, lettuce and tomatoes as well as rhubarb and strawberries (which were my favourite and seemed much sweeter in those days to the ones we buy in supermarkets now).

One of our other regular merchants was Ernie, the fruiterer. Ernie was of Italian extraction, he had an outgoing personality and was a firm favourite with the kids as he would often cut up an apple or slice a piece of fruit for us kids to eat (this most likely stopped us from 'pinching' things off his cart!).

There was a song us kids used to sing in those days about a 'wee tallie' ('tallie' being the slang for Italians) which I always associated with Ernie. It wasn't very long and had a slightly rude connotation, which is most probably why we sang it.

"In yonder green valley, there live a wee tallie,
                I gave him some biscuits to start a wee shop,
        but when the shop started, the wee tallie farted
                and sent all the biscuits away up a kye …"

If parents were around we would mumble the offending word unless we felt very game, then we'd blurt it out and run off giggling! I have no idea where this song came from, but there were many songs in a similar vein which we sang as kids when playing in the streets, some were handed down through parents, grandparents and friends, such as the one about abstinence from drink.

Glasgow was a working man's city and drink was often the only release men had from the everyday drudgery of work and the poverty of home life – though it was often the women and children who suffered most.

'Vote No Licence for Me' was most probably from my parents' time or earlier, and was an attempt to stop the granting of a liqueur licence to an area. (it may have come from the temperance society)

> "Vote no licence for me, vote no licence for me,
>> the children all cry keep Whiteinch dry
>> and vote no licence for me"

(Whiteinch was a suburb of Glasgow between Partick and Scotstoun)

Houses in the late '40s did not have the 'white goods' that are commonplace today; we had no fridges or washing machines and food was kept in a pantry. Cooking was mainly with gas and households were heated by an open coal fire while sometimes there would be a smaller gas fire in the bedrooms.

I can recall when we moved to our first own house in Dykebar Avenue, getting up in the dark in the winter and getting dressed for school in front of our gas fire in the bedroom that my brother and I shared.

In winter, we'd go to bed with a stone hot water bottle to warm our blankets and our feet (and quite often we'd wear socks to bed to help keep warm – though sleeping two or three to a bed also helped!).

One of the most fascinating places in my granny's house, in Scotstoun, was the 'glory hole'. This was like a small room underneath the house, just outside the pantry, which we entered by lifting a trapdoor and going down three or four steps into the 'glory hole'. This area got its name as it was where the family kept all their valuable items such as wedding gifts, or the females of the family's 'glory boxes' (special items they had bought in anticipation of marriage). The 'glory hole' was also a place where Christmas presents were hidden from us kids…one reason I liked to explore the area any chance I got!

Our backyards were great playing areas in the late '40s, especially for games like 'hide-and-seek', as not only did we have garden sheds but some air raid shelters were still remaining from the war while the coal bunker (situated along the back of the house) made an excellent hiding place…as long as you didn't use it on coal delivery day. This happened to me once; I don't know who got the biggest fright, the coalman or me as he nearly tipped a full bag of coal over the top of me! I stayed out of the bunkers for some time after that!

The families of the street were a close-knit community as well as everyone knowing everyone else's business, neighbours were very much into caring and sharing and had real empathy for those who were down on their luck or had misfortune befall them. There was also great respect shown to neighbours at certain events, none more so than when there was a death in the family. On such occasions, the whole street would draw their blinds as a mark of respect and these would remain closed until after the funeral. The kids would be kept indoors and were not to be seen or heard…

Weddings, however, were just the opposite and the whole street would join in the celebrations…especially when it came to the bride and groom throwing pennies out of the wedding car (usually a taxi) window to the shouts of "Hard up! Hard up!" This was an old Scottish custom that had the 'newlyweds' sharing their wealth with those less fortunate, hence the cry from the crowd of "Hard up!" (if you were 'hard up' you were battling to make ends meet). With the shower of pennies coming through the air, kids (and adults) would scramble to get as many coins as they could lay their hands on…a few pennies could keep you in lollies for weeks and the skinned elbows and knees from the scuffles on the footpath were all part of the fun!

Birthday parties were another highlight for those who could afford them and us kids would try to keep onside with those whose birthdays were coming up in the hope of getting an invitation to their party. We had a boy at the top of our street whose Mum always gave him the best birthday parties and while my pal George (who lived across the road from him) always got an invite, I usually missed out.

I was somewhat seen as an 'undesirable', due to no doubt to my attitude towards this mothers' son, who, in the Glasgow dialect, was a bit of a 'jessie'…thus missing out on his birthday parties was something I just had to live with…but there were other compensations like Halloween and Guy Fawkes Night, two of the best days of the year for kids outside of Christmas!

Halloween was very big in Scotland; the celebrations dating back from the days when people believed in evil spirits, witches and fairies. The 'Hallowed Evening' (Hallowe'en) was the night before All Saints Day and the villagers and farmers would leave food outside of their homes to appease the spirits. From this grew the custom of Halloween; the American 'trick or treat' is a pale version of the Scottish celebration.

Us kids would be practising our 'party pieces' for weeks leading up to Halloween (31 October) as well as discussing what fancy dress we'd wear. The boys would always be pirates, ghosts, cowboys or Indians while the girls would be 'witches' or 'fairies'. The week before we'd hollow out our turnips (never pumpkins) cut a face in them and find a candle that would fit inside and light the face up without giving off too much smoke.

On the night our gang of boys and girls would go to every house in the street, knock on the door and when it was opened, say in our best voices, "Please may we have our Halloween?" Most folks would then invite us in out of the cold (those who didn't were the ones that got firecrackers through their letterbox on Guy Fawkes Night!) and in front of a blazing fire we'd all perform our party pieces; some would sing, some dance and some recite poetry.

After complimenting us on our performances, the folks would reward us with sweets, apples or oranges, nuts, and if lucky a threepenny bit, sometimes we'd also be given a 'hot toddy' of mulled ale; this was usually a mug of cider with a hot poker from the fire thrust into it to 'mull' the liquid and when you drank it you could feel the warmth through your whole body – it fortified you for your trip back out into the frosty night! With a 'Thank you!' we'd be off to the next house.

At the end of the night, it was like Christmas as we emptied out our pillowslips to see what we'd gathered. Mostly we'd have enough sweets and 'goodies' to last us till the Festive Season and with a bit of luck enough three penny pieces to buy extra fireworks for Guy Fawkes Night!

Halloween parties were also great fun, where such games as 'dooking for apples' and 'treacle scones' followed by each adult and child doing a party piece, would keep us going for hours; the night just seemed to slip away and in no time it was time for home and Halloween would be over for another year.

Glasgow's 'city bakers' used to make a special cake for Halloween; a round sponge cake with orange icing with a big 'smiley' face. These were very popular and became so well known that people with round faces and big smiles would often be spoken as having a face 'like a city baker's Halloween cake'!

We'd only just be getting over the excitement of Halloween when Guy Fawkes Night was upon us (5 November). Guy Fawkes was one of a group of Catholics who tried to blow up the houses of parliament in the early 1600s to do away with the then government; he was caught and hanged…The fireworks on 5 November are symbolic of his attempt and the 'guy' on the bonfire of how he ended up!

Again, us kids would have been working towards this night for weeks, gathering old bits of wood, old furniture and motor car tyres, in fact, anything that would burn and bringing it to the site of our bonfire at the open ground behind the high school. The bonfire was the meeting place for all in the neighbourhood and the whole family would be there to watch and join the show on Guy Fawkes Night. The night always started off with the ceremony of lighting the bonfire then the 'guy' would be thrown on the top and we'd all yell and scream as we watched 'him' burn.

And we all had fireworks to let off! Roman candles, Catherine wheels, skyrockets, volcanoes but the most popular with the boys were the tuppeny bungers and the jumping jacks (strings of little bungers tied together which exploded all over the place). We would terrorise the neighbourhood leading up to the night with 'bungers' exploding in letterboxes, dustbins and pillar boxes (which quite often ruined Her Majesty's Mail!).

A favourite trick was to knock on the door of a neighbour we didn't like and leave a 'bunger' fizzing on their doorstep. When the door opened and our timing was right, the 'bunger' would explode at their feet and we'd run off down the street howling with glee!!! Now and again one of us kids would get burnt by a firework (most likely the reason why kids aren't allowed fireworks today); this usually was through throwing 'bungers' at one and other or having 'shoot outs' with roman candles.

This latter 'game' was quite dangerous as we would hold a roman candle in our hands light the wick and 'fire' the exploding balls at one and other, pretending we were our favourite cowboys…and there was always the 'eijit'(idiot) now and again who would drop a 'bunger' into someone box of fireworks and the whole lot would go off with a bang, with skyrockets and Catherine wheels flying everywhere! If we survived Guy Fawkes Night, Christmas and school holidays were soon upon us and we were in winter…

Easter was another great time for kids and although a religious festival, it was always enjoyed because of the festivities that came with it. Easter marked springtime in Scotland and everywhere the leaves would be coming out on the trees and the spring bulbs would be pushing up through the gardens, the parks would be a mass of colour with daffodils and jonquils bending in the breeze.

Near where we lived in Scotstoun was a large park known to us as Whiteinch Park, it was a favourite place for families to go walking and have picnics. We often used to go there at Easter time and roll our Easter eggs down the grassy hill. Our Easter eggs were always 'homemade', we'd hard boil the eggs then paint the shells with different designs. When we rolled the eggs down the hill, they would often hit a stone or rock and split open. This activity related to the Easter celebration of the resurrection of Christ as the egg represented the stone being rolled away from the tomb.

Whiteinch Park also had some large lakes, which were used for sailing model yachts, and the streams which fed these were the homes of a small fish called a 'stickleback'. These small fish, similar to minnows, but with a bright red belly and three spines on their back (hence the name) were a 'poor mans' goldfish. I'd often go there with my fishnet and jelly jar to try and catch one for a pet. Sticklebacks, or 'baggy minnows' as they were sometimes called, could live for months quite comfortably in a jam jar with a bit of pondweed and be fed on bread crumbs, and when you found them floating 'belly up' it was off to the park to catch a few more!

One day while I was 'fishing', I was pushed into the pond by a big kid...I don't know who got the biggest fright, me or the sticklebacks! Luckily Mum was close at hand and pulled me out, as at that stage I couldn't swim. It was a very wet and bedraggled 'fisherman' who went home empty-handed that day!

Whiteinch Park was also famous for its fossil grove; this was a group of fossilised trees which were in an enclosed area. As kids, we used to love being taken there and imagining that dinosaurs and cavemen were lurking among the huge ferns that grew around the fossils.

It was in this period too that Mum took me to see my first picture, the Walt Disney animated film '*Lady and the Tramp*'. I was fascinated by it and I'm sure it had something to do with me wanting to become a cartoonist when I grew up. The other film I recall was the '48 film '*The Red Shoes*' about a ballet dancer who was murdered, which gave me nightmares!!! I don't recall going to any other pictures after that until the Saturday morning matinees with my pals, where the rootin'-tootin' cowboys were much easier to relate to.

1950s – Street Games,
Chittering Bites, Television and Specs

In late '50, our family moved from Harefield Drive in Scotstoun to Dykebar Avenue in Knightswood where Dad took up his new position of Warden of the Knightswood Community Centre.

At last, we had a house of our own, just as well as our family, had now grown to five; my youngest sister, Fiona, was born in April of the following year. Our new home was similar to Gran Marshal's, except that we were now in the upstairs section of a semi-detached house. Alistair and I shared a bedroom while Lana was in the smaller bedroom next to the master bedroom. In addition, we had a living/dining room a kitchen with a pantry and a bathroom…and all to ourselves!…and we had a telephone for the first time!

Dad's work was only two minutes away at the bottom of our street, while my new primary school, Bankhead, was five minutes in the other direction. Bankhead school was bombed during the Clydbank blitz of '41, which was before my time. An interesting book was written on this period of the school's history in '01. Bankhead was Alastair's first school.

However, I, being five years older than Alastair, had little to do with him, or my sisters for that matter, as we grew up. My most vivid recollection involving them was when Dad took us in a taxi to collect Mum and Fiona from the nursing home near Anniesland Cross after Fiona's birth; it was the first time I'd been in a taxi!

I was in my seventh year when we moved to Knightswood and I soon made friends with the other kids in the street. My two closest pals were Brian (Cheyne) and Barry (Patrick) Brian was a couple of years older than me while Barry, only a few months but we were inseparable in most things, however, they would always put me through the 'third degree' before letting me into our street gang's clubhouse!

The clubhouse (which was a shed in Barry's backyard) was where we held our secret meetings and planned our activities. We were right into secret passwords and taking oaths and the 'den' was always shrouded in mystery and lit by candles and there were always kids in the street who were banned from the secret meetings for all sorts of reasons, never however Barry or Brian! There was one of the girls in the street, Jeannie (Brown) who always seemed to be a member of the gang, whether this was because of her willingness to play 'doctors and nurses' I'm not sure, but it got to me that she was always allowed into the den whether she knew the passwords or not, while I was often refused entry because I forgot the password or Barry would change it without letting us know!

There was, however, one family of boys who were never in the club; they were the Murphy boys, good Irish Catholics! Not that this seemed to worry them as they could hold their own in any of the games we played…and when it came to fighting, you didn't mix it with the Murphys!

In the '50s, there was still quite some feeling in Glasgow between the Catholics and the Protestants, this always came to the fore when the 'auld firm' (Rangers and Celtic football teams) came together – it was many years before a Catholic could play for Rangers and vice versa.

I recall my one and only visit to the 'fitba' (football/soccer) when Rangers and Celtic were playing. Dad's brother, Uncle Roy, picked me up on his motorbike from Whiteinch Park, where I'd been fishing for 'baggy minnows'. The ride home was exciting enough as my uncle raced his bike home with me on the back and my 'jelly jar' of minnows spilling water all the way…we got to my place with just enough water in the jar for the minnows to survive! Then it was off to the fitba.

Uncle Roy got tickets for the middle section of the stands. This meant that the Rangers supporters were on one side of us and the Celtic supporters on the other…my uncle thought this was the safest place to be…how wrong he was! When one team scored (I can't remember which team) empty beer bottles flew through the air towards the opposing supporters, unfortunately for the 'non-aligned' in between none of the bottles reached the opposition and these rained down on us! This happened every time one of the teams scored…it was my first and last visit to a football game!

Our street was an example of the segregation of the religions (whether planned or by accident, I don't know), with the Catholic families mainly down one end and the 'Proddies' down the other; as Dad worked with all of the community we were in the middle!

The streets were our playground, more so than our backyards, and especially in summer time when we'd be out playing till well after 10 o'clock at night. With no cars to worry about we'd play our games of 'kick the can', 'release', 'statues' and 'hide-and-seek' till we were tired out.

Among many games we played including: 'What's the Time Mr Wolf?' and 'Ali Baba whose got the ball?', 'cowboys and Indians' was by far the favourite. While the road was used for these games as well as a variety of ball games like 'heedies' (headers) and 'brandings', we also took over the footpaths for skipping (in which both boys and girls competed) and 'peever' (hopscotch). Our peevers were usually of flat boot polish tins filled with the earth which was excellent for skidding along the footpaths. Our different games chalked out on the footpaths would remain there until such time as the rain washed them out or they were worn off. Games chalked out on favourite positions would be gone over time and time again and would sometimes remain in same place for months.

Marbles (or 'jorries') was also popular as was the playing of 'conkers'. The most highly sought after marbles were the 'steelies'; these were steel ball bearings which could smash 'jorries' to pieces. To win a 'steelie' off a pal you had to win at least three games in a row. Conkers was a game played with chestnuts on a string with the aim being to smash your opponent's conker with yours; each time you were victorious with your conker it gained in stature. Some boys' conkers were reputed to be winners of over a hundred clashes.

We all had secrets as to how to make our chestnut invincible, all would be roasted firstly to harden them, then some would be steeped in vinegar or similar substances to improve them further…sometimes it worked and sometimes it didn't, but it was always a sad day when your number one 'conker' was smashed to smithereens by an opponent!

In the chestnut season, us kids would roam far and wide seeking the best trees with the biggest chestnuts…and these were usually on private land; not that that stopped us! We were often to be seen scampering for our lives with pockets bulging with 'conkers' and being chased by irate landowners!

On the quieter side, we'd swap comics, cigarette cards and bubble-gum cards or even 'scraps'. 'Scraps' were a great pastime, though mainly with the girls; you would buy a sheet of scraps from the paper shop (these were usually kept between the pages of a notebook or such) and swap your duplicates for ones you didn't have. 'Scraps' were beautifully glossy coloured pictures of all sorts of things, the favourites being angels, cherubs and Santa Claus. Some would come in sets and would range from about two inches high to six or eight inches; these were highly prized. They were most likely the forerunners of today's stickers but of a much higher quality although because they were made of paper they could tear easily, which made them worthless unless hard to replace, then they could retain some value.

Our favourite comics were the '*Beano*' and '*Dandy*' with the football comics '*Hotspur*' and '*Rover*' not far behind. Cowboy comics were also read avidly and swapped around until in many cases they fell to pieces.

The other interest in our early years was collecting and boys especially got involved in this. We'd collect all manner of things, such as tram, bus and train numbers as well as bird's eggs and butterflies (conservation was not on the agenda then!). It was not unusual to see a group of youngsters standing on a bus route or on a railway bridge gathering the numbers of the buses and trains as they went by. Trolleybuses were a favourite for a time but like the buses themselves, went out of fashion.

I couldn't understand the demise of the trolley bus as it was so much quieter than either the trams or buses and gave a very comfortable ride, and they could weave in and out of the traffic unlike trams (though you couldn't put your halfpenny on the rails and have it flattened out to a penny size like you could with tramlines! Maybe that was it!).

Perhaps most common in our collecting were stamps, 'tin soldiers' (soldiers also included cowboys and Indians as well as knights in armour and on horseback) and cigarette cards, which usually depicted football players, though there were some which had photos of scenery of Scotland. In later years, such cards were 'giveaways' in bubble gum packs.

We also used to play a game, the name of which I can't remember, based on the names of cigarettes. We'd have two teams; one team would tell a story, included in it somewhere would be the name of the cigarette and the other team would have to guess the name. Names such as 'senior service', 'passing cloud', 'wills woodbine' etc. would easily be detected but some of the lesser known brands (and there were plenty of them in those days) would have us guessing for ages!

Stamp albums were very popular and this may have been because the British Empire still held sway and we obtained many stamps from countries of the Empire. All of my pals collected stamps and some had quite impressive albums.

Of course, we wouldn't be kids if we didn't get up to some mischief and this usually involved upsetting the neighbours! One of our neighbours had a lovely crab apple tree and when it was in the fruit we'd raid it. While the apples weren't great eating, it was the thrill of the chase that made it a game for us as we'd often be caught in the act and Mr Jones would come flying out of his house and onto our tails!…and while we were seldom caught, if our parents were told of the incident, we'd get a belting…and I got my share!

On another occasion, my pal Brian (Morton) and I were out playing at night with torches and we decided to hide in the bushes of a small park near the main road and shine our torches at motorists as they came out of a side street and onto the main road. We thought this great fun as we watched motorists shield their eyes while trying to negotiate the corner – luckily no accident occurred and no one got hurt from this very foolish prank…no one except us, that is, as one motorist (unsighted by us) got out of his car behind us and grabbed us both by the scruff of the neck and gave us a couple of cuffs around the ears! He told us how stupid and dangerous our actions were and took our torches from us. Suitably chastised, our only consolation was that our parents weren't told so we escaped further hiding!

Most likely the worst mischief (if you could call it that) we got up to was with the trains and the shunting yard just near where we lived. At the end of their shift, the trains would be driven into the shunting yards; this entailed the drivers' offsider jumping off the train (the train would only be travelling at a snails' pace) and pulling a lever at the trackside which changed the train from the main line onto the shunting yard line, then he'd jump back on the train as it went past him and into the yard.

Sometimes we'd jam a brick or similar in between the rails where the lever was, which stopped the tracks from aligning properly; when the train reached this section of track it would get a jolt. On one occasion our jamming of the points caused the train to 'jump' the track! We took off like frightened rabbits! None of us ever tried this 'trick' again and for months we were sure the 'polis' would come and get us! A lesser bit of mischief was our game of trying to drop a brown paper bag full of flour down the funnel of a train as it passed under the bridge! We never knew the outcome of this even when we scored a direct hit!

It wasn't only neighbours and grown-ups we'd play tricks on, some of our worst escapades were reserved for our pals, like the use of 'itchy coos' and stink bombs. 'Itchy coos' were the seeds of a small garden rose, which when you opened up its seed pods were full of tiny hairs. These seedpods would be pushed down the back of an unsuspecting target, between his shirt and skin and rubbed hard, the result was agony! The victim would be itching for hours afterwards or until he could take his shirt off and get rid of the offending hairs.

Stink bombs were used in all sorts of situations and their rotten egg smell would have the victim(s) gasping for air! Woe betide you if you were caught with stink bombs on you, your so-called pals would take great delight in crushing them in your pockets and you would smell to high heaven for the rest of the day! Worst still, if you were found out to be the culprit of a stink bomb attack in school, it would be six of the best at the very least!

As kids growing up our pets were quite different from those of children nowadays; there were fewer cats and dogs around. Dogs especially were not a common household pet (perhaps because they took up a considerable amount of space and were big eaters). None of my pals ever had a dog, our pets were mainly of the smaller variety such as goldfish, guinea pigs, rabbits, mice and budgies or canaries. On occasions, we'd gain a hedgehog as a pet, but they always remained wild and would forage in the garden and under the hedgerows, coming to us mainly for titbits of food and would eventually move on.

There was always a bit of a commotion when a pal down the street would be found with your hedgehog! The other unusual pet which was quite common in houses was a tortoise; Gran Waddell had one (Tammy) which lived in the hearth in front of her living room fire. It spent most of its time sleeping and eating lettuce leaves and vegetable scraps. Us kids (or I) would sometimes prod Tammy to try and get him (we presumed it was a 'him', we never found out!) to move, but we had to be careful because while he may have been slow at walking, he could stretch out his neck and give you a nasty nip with his 'beak' quick as a flash! On more than one occasion he drew blood from me!

My first pets were a pair of budgies, which Dad bought me when we lived at Dykebar Avenue. The budgies seemed very pally towards each other and we thought nothing of it until one day we found eggs on the bottom of their cage! Our birds had mated! This started me off as a breeder! Dad helped me build a nesting box for the birds, and soon I was giving away baby budgies to family and friends! Mind you, it was Mum who did most of the looking after of the 'chicks';

I would often come home from school and find Mum with a blanket on the living room floor 'feeding' half a dozen squawking chicks with an eyedropper full of milk or similar concoction! (I think Mum was glad when I progressed to guinea pigs!)

By this stage of my life, Dad had allocated me certain chores around the house which I had to carry out if I wanted to receive my pocket money. While we all helped with such tasks as washing up (no dishwashers in those days) and making our beds, my other task was weeding the garden…which I loathed.

Dad was keen on his garden, but with his work never seemed to have time to look after it properly, so it fell to me. Here was me who hated vegetables having to tend to them! The weeds seemed to grow prolifically and I'd no sooner be finished one section of the garden and the next had to be done again. Dad would come home at night and inspect my work and he'd often find a patch I'd missed or had just turned the ground over without pulling out the weeds…and I'd have to do it all again, or no pocket money! (a threat that was seldom if ever carried out)

Onion grass was the bane of my life. I'd pull a plant out and if not done with care the little 'onion' seeds would fall everywhere and within a week I'd have twice as much onion grass as when I started! When first given this chore, I would often dig up the plants instead of the weeds as I was somewhat unsure of what was what (they all looked the same to me) and also in the forlorn hope that Dad may relieve me of the task…no chance!

Patiently at first, Dad would point out that weeds had one long root while plants had (usually) several short or surface roots. This was knocked into my head with one or two cuffs around the ears, latterly! (In later life, I was to become quite a keen gardener, thanks to this early training!)

My other main chore was the cleaning out of the hearth each morning during the colder months and preparing the fire to be lit in the evening. This was a simple enough task, the only drawback being taking the ashes outside on a cold winter morning. I enjoyed the open fires in winter as they not only warmed up the house but we were allowed to toast our bread against the glowing coals (with marshmallows if we were lucky!).

I was never what one would call a 'good child', mind you. I doubt that I was any better or worse than most of my pals, but I recall Mum would often threaten me after a misdemeanour with "Just you wait till your father gets home!" I'd spend the rest of the day in fear and trepidation waiting for Dad's homecoming!

Often Dad would be home late in the evening and when Mum would tell him he needed to deal with me, Dad would ask her what for…and she'd have forgotten! I got out of many 'skelpings' that way as Dad would give me a talking to, though sometimes I think I would have preferred a few cuffs around the head!

One such incident involved my cousin, Donald, who I had to play with whenever he came to visit. (Donald was the same age as my brother, Alastair, and I was always looking for ways to get out of this role; how Alastair got out of it I never worked out!)

On this occasion in an attempt to get away from him, I suggested we play hide-and-seek, provided I got to hide firstly, to which Donald agreed. I ran around the back of our house, jumped the neighbour's fence and was back in the house and upstairs in my bedroom before Donald finished counting. Donald was wandering around the backyard calling my name, which I knew would bring Mum and I'd have to play with him again. I don't know what got into me, but I filled a bucket with water from our bathroom, and as he passed underneath my bedroom window I threw it all over him! He got soaked! He came into the house dripping wet and crying and of course, his mum, Aunt Greta, went spare! I was sitting in my bedroom reading a comic when Mum and my aunt burst in and I denied all knowledge of how Donald got wet…Mum just said, "You wait till your Dad gets home!"

For a while, I went along to the local Sunday school which was in the church just opposite the community centre. While I quite enjoyed the bible stories and the singing, I didn't last long. I must say though, that some of the 'songs' that we learned stayed with me such as 'Jesus bids us shine with a pure clean light' and 'Running over, running over, my cups full and running over'. However, the one that stuck in my mind most was the ditty 'Big ones, small ones everybody come, join the darkies Sunday school…bring a stick of chewing gum and stick it on the floor and we'll tell you Bible stories that you've never heard before!'…not quite the Sunday school ethic!

Mum often said that while I was the only one in the family christened, I was the worst of the lot! My father (not Dad) and his family had been very involved with religion. When we visited his brother, Uncle Jack, and his family, which thankfully was not often, we were not allowed to go outside and play which made for a very boring Sunday afternoon. It was on these occasions that I learned to appreciate Dad taking us climbing in the Campsie Fells on weekends.

I attended Bankhead Primary School from '51 till '56, where I was more interested in getting picked by the teacher to deliver the milk crates to the classrooms and having competitions with my pals to see who could drink the most milk in the shortest time than I was in lessons. Schools were provided with third of a pint bottle of milk for every student; these were usually given out at the morning play break. (This was part of a programme by the Glasgow Corporation to build stronger and healthier children after the war years.)

The boys of the class would all compete for the teacher's favour to be given the role of delivering the milk (as this got you out of the last lesson before the break!). It needed two boys to carry out the task and there would always be milk left over which was then consumed by those delivering the milk.

As kids we were always on the lookout for extra sustenance, whether this was because of the war years or that there never seemed enough food to go around, I'm not sure. At lunchtimes, there would always be kids who hovered around seeking a bite of your 'jeely piece' or some of your lunch that you didn't want (which wasn't often the case) or they'd 'bag your dumps' which was an expression for being given your apple core to eat after you'd finished eating the apple. I have no idea where the expression came from but it was in regular use throughout my schooldays.

I did, however, excel in one area in my time at Bankhead school and that was in writing. We still had inkwells and wrote with wooden pens with nibs and it was quite easy, if you weren't careful, to 'blot your copybook' with a smudge of the ink off your pen. We would practice daily at refining our copperplate writing with light upstrokes and heavy downstrokes. I was often held up as an example to the class as to how writing should be done. I went on to win a number of our classroom and school competitions with my writing (this all came undone however when in later life I attended college and my writing became a scribble as I tried in vain to keep up with the workload!).

It was at Bankhead also, where I learned a lesson in 'honesty'. I had been involved in a prank for which somehow, one of the girls in the class was about to be punished. I owned up that it was me who was responsible and not the female class member. To my surprise, the teacher praised me to the class for being honest and let me off without punishment. This stuck with me for the rest of my school years…though it didn't always work in my favour!

The thing I liked most about Bankhead was the Christmas pageants that all classes took part in. The rehearsals for these would commence around mid-

November and each class would have at least two plays or skits, which they would perform in front of all classes, come December. While I was never picked to take part in these, I loved to watch the performances and my mind would wander towards Christmas.

It was also at Bankhead that my eyesight went on me, quite suddenly. One day, I was sitting up near the back of the classroom when the teacher asked me to read from the blackboard. When I tried I couldn't make out what was written as it appeared 'fuzzy'. At first, the teacher thought I was fooling, but then realising I was having trouble, arranged for an eye test. I had become short-sighted!

When I turned up at school the next week in glasses, the name-calling started. "Hey! Four eyes!", "Specky!", "Skelly eyes!", "Goggly eyes!", "Gocky!"…I would trade insult with insult, but would usually end up trading punches! Glasses in those days were a circle in wire frames and had no aesthetic appeal what so ever; mind you, maybe they were before their time as they were similar to those worn by the 'Beatle' John Lennon in later years, and Harry Potter gave them a comeback in the films of the early 2000s.

I was quite pugnacious (whether due to my wearing of glasses or not I'm not sure). I recall having an altercation with a classmate, Frank (Caddell) and I hit him square on the nose with my best punch; Frank just blinked his eyes and looked at me, but didn't retaliate. Frank would remind me of this incident in years to come when we were both at Victoria Drive School; by that time he had become a strapping big lad who towered over me – luckily he didn't hold a grudge!

If Dad was on duty at the community centre at the weekend, I was able to join my pals at the local picture house, provided I could get Dad to increase my pocket money! On Saturday morning, we'd catch the tram or bus to Anniesland Cross where the Odeon picture house would have a morning show for the kids. It cost a shilling to get in and we'd buy a bag of sweeties to enjoy during the show.

Once inside we were in our element, along with a theatre full of kids. The show started when 'Uncle Harry' came on stage and told us the programme for the morning, this would be interspersed with a few wisecracks then he'd get us all to sing along with the bouncing ball on the movie screen. A couple of hundred kids would be singing their heads off to *Mocking Bird Hill*' or '*On top of old smoky'* while at the same time throwing aniseed balls or firing pea shooters at other kids!

When we finished our sweeties we'd blow up the paper bag they were in and 'bang' them with our fists…if this was done at an exciting time during the movies there would be squeals all over the theatre…and if we got caught we were thrown out!

The movie show would commence with one or two cartoons and we'd be laughing our heads off at *'Heckle and Jeckle'* or *'Popeye'*, but the theatre would go quiet when the main feature came on. This would be a serial with *'Tarzan'* or a cowboy adventure such as *'Gene Autry and the Thunder Riders'*. Once this was underway, we'd all be yelling and booing the 'baddies' and screaming for the 'goodies' to watch their backs! The serial would always end with the hero being thrown over a cliff or tied up in a building that was about to be blown up; then the voice on the screen would intone, "Will our hero escape from this awful fate? Don't miss next week's exciting episode!"…and of course, quite often I did and I'd be at my pal's to bring me up to date on the happenings.

Cowboys were the favourite movie characters of the day and our heroes such as Tom Mix, Roy Rogers and Hopalong Cassidy made regular appearances on the big screen. While Roy Rogers was the hero to most, I preferred Hopalong Cassidy as he was more a 'man's man' to me and looked the part in his black outfit, whereas Roy was always singing soppy songs and getting caught up with the females.

Playing 'cowboys and Indians' was our favourite pastime and we'd often relive what we'd seen at the movies in our street games. We would also make our own guns and bows and arrows out of wood and tree branches. The latter could be quite dangerous as our arrows were made out of bamboo and could be shot quite a distance, the 'cowboys' always knew when and 'Indian' had got them!…and more than once one of us had to be treated after being 'shot' with an arrow! Catapults and spears, as well as swords and shields, were also part of our armoury depending on the game we were playing…in those days kids lived dangerously! As well as homemade guns, (some of which 'fired' elastic bands) most of my pals had an array of bought 'six-shooters' (some of which fired 'caps' and some slug pellets or potato pellets).

I'd sometimes get a loan of one or two from my pals, but because of Dad's attitude towards guns I'd have to hide them; this was always getting me into trouble. One time Dad found my 'borrowed' guns hidden under the coal bunker

(I never thought he'd be looking under that for anything!)…it was back to playing cowboys & Indians using my fingers for my six guns!

Speaking of songs that kids sang at the picture house, there was also another whole group of songs which kids sang as they played on the streets, some which were part of skipping games; like 'Christopher Columbus' or 'the big ship sails up the eilly alley oh' and others which were party games, as in 'bee-baw babbity' or 'farmer in the dell' which were action songs. Others still were sung for no reason at all and their background is obscure, but we all knew them and loved to sing them sometimes at the most inappropriate moments.

"Ye canny shove yer grannie aff a bus" was one of the most popular (maybe they came through vaudeville or the pantomimes):

"Ye canny shove yer grannie aff a bus,
　naw, ye canny shove yer grannie aff a bus,
Ye canny shove yer grannie, fur she's yer mammy's mammy,
　naw, ye canny shove yer grannie aff a bus!"

'Skinny malinky long legs' was another, often sang when a person with big feet walked past….

"Skinny malinky long legs, big banana feet,
went tae the pictures an' fell through the seat
When the pictured started, skinny-malinky farted,
When the picture ended, skinny-malinky bended"

If this was sung when a man went past, quite often you'd have to get off your mark quick, as with an exclamation like "You cheeky wee devils!", he'd be off after you!

Another sung with gusto when decrying someone else's house or their lodger was:

"Oor wee hoose, is the best wee hoose,
the best wee hoose in Glesga
The only thing whit's wrang wi' it
is baldy-heided maister!"

"*Wee chookie birdie*" is another I remember well, though this was more in keeping with nursery rhymes and was often sung to a small child to soothe them down.

Dad was never keen on any of his family spending time in indoor activities (apart from swimming) or going to the pictures for that matter, so once he had established himself in his new position at the Knightswood Community Centre he'd take Alastair and I away at the weekends to climb in the Campsie Fells, the hills just outside Glasgow, along with any of my pals who wanted to join us. Brian and Barry would often come along on these days.

In his younger days, Dad had been a member of the junior mountaineering club of Scotland and with his pals had climbed and mountaineered all over Scotland, as well as England and Wales. One of Dad's group was Tom Weir who was to become a well-known writer on mountaineering and a journalist with *Glasgow's Sunday Post* newspaper. Dad's background in climbing made him keen for Alastair and me to gain an appreciation of the Scottish countryside.

As we got older Dad would take us further into the highlands and we'd spend weekends away climbing and staying at youth hostels overnight. The youth hostels were a great experience as not only were we bunked in with other hikers, but you had to learn to fend for yourself in cooking as well as 'home maintenance'.

Though we didn't always appreciate it at the time (especially when we were trudging through knee-deep snow with a blizzard in our faces), those excursions into the hills of Scotland were part of a wonderful childhood where the good times far outweighed the bad. Every climb was an experience and with the Scottish weather you could never be sure of what you'd encounter, often we'd have four seasons in the space of an hour, never mind a day!

Often we would carry a pair of ice skates in our haversacks in wintertime and would spend time skating on the frozen lochans up in the hills. Our haversacks were also improvised as toboggans where there were gentle slopes we could slide down, which was great fun and added to the enjoyment of the day. Although it was now almost a decade since the war ended, we would still find parts of shot down aeroplanes up in the hills, some of the wreckage would be large enough to play in which gave us a break from struggling through snowdrifts at times.

We would occasionally meet some of Dad's old pals on our hikes and they'd stop and have hot cocoa and relive past memories. This was most appreciated one winter's day when Alastair and I were feeling the going pretty tough, trudging through snowfalls two and three feet deep when we crossed paths with one of Dad's old pals who was snuggled behind a rockface keeping out of the weather. He was drinking hot chocolate and eating marshmallow biscuits, Alastair and I didn't need a second invitation when he invited us to share his repast!

Over the years we climbed many of the hills and mountains around Loch Lomond side and the Trossachs including the quite hard climbs of 'The Cobbler' and Ben Nevis, but most of our climbs or more correctly, rambles were on the Campsie Fells which were right at our backdoor in Glasgow. It was on one of their smaller rock faces that Dad introduced me to rock climbing with a rope and my first experience was quite dramatic, for me at least as I climbed 'hands and knees' up a chimney in the rocks. Though the chimney was only about twenty feet in length, I was very pleased when I reached the top and was able to climb out onto the rock platform.

While we had a few unsettling moments during our years of climbing, our worst incident happened when we were in the foothills around Dumbarton. We had just passed through a farmyard, walking on a right of way (in Scotland there is no trespassing law) when we were accosted by a fellow and a large Alsatian dog. This fellow told us we were trespassing and to get off the hillside.

Dad, knowing the rights of climbers, remonstrated with the chap who threatened to set the dog on us and call in his companions (who we could see further up the hills, and they also had dogs) if we didn't retrace our steps at once. I could see Dad was livid and I'm sure he would have forced the issue if he'd had some grown-ups with him, but as he only has Alastair and me and a couple of my pals, common sense prevailed and we returned down the mountainside – no hiking for us on that day!

That incident was the closest I'd heard to Dad swear, in fact, none of us kids ever heard Dad swear while we were growing up, 'damn' was the closest he came to swearing, at least within our earshot. While Glasgow (George Square) was a great place for swearers, it was a definite 'no-no' at our place. I can remember vividly Mum castigating me the first time she heard me say "shut up!" (shurrup in Glaswegian)…how the world has changed!

In '52, Dad bought a second-hand Morris van (one of the first cars in our street) which gave us greater access to the countryside and trips to Loch Lomond and the Trossachs and their surrounding hills became a regular event. We were at Loch Lomond for a picnic with the whole family not long after Dad bought the Morris when we had our first encounter with a 'road hog'.

Dad was just pulling out onto the road from our picnic area when this motorbike and sidecar came hurtling round the bend at such a speed that the rider didn't have time to avoid us, but somehow he managed to lean the bike over on its side and as we watched from inside our van in amazement. The sidecar's wheel travelled the length of the van's side before thumping back down onto the ground disappearing with the motorbike in a cloud of exhaust fumes! We were left dazed but unhurt and marvelling at our lucky escape. Dad was more cautious in future when exiting many of the hidden roadside areas around Loch Lomond.

Swimming was Dad's other great love and most Thursday nights he would take Al and me along with any of my pals who wanted to come, down to the local corporation baths at Whiteinch. While we both could swim by this time, Dad was keen to see us improve; he was always talking about Al or I becoming as good as Johnny Weismuller. (I often wondered who Johnny Weiss mother was and how come she was such a good swimmer! It was some time before I realised that he was talking about the guy who played Tarzan in the movies!)

While my pals would be having fun playing 'tag' or seeing who could swim the furthest underwater, Dad would always make Al and me do a set number of lengths of the pool before allowing us to join in the fun. Al would often hide in the hot tubs area of the baths (where you showered or bathed before entering the pool) and Dad would not be able to see him because of the steam! Although Al was a good swimmer, he loved the hot tubs and as soon as Dad's back was turned he'd be out of the pool and back into the tubs!

The best thing about Thursday nights was the 'chittering bite' after our swim, Dad would always have some chocolate or similar for us to eat when we came out of the baths with the concept that once you had something in your mouth, especially on the colds winter nights, your teeth would stop chattering! (hence the name 'chittering bite').

Often Dad would buy each of us packets of Smiths Crisps and we'd 'dive' into the packet looking for the little twist of blue greaseproof paper, which held the salt (pre-salted crisps had not been developed yet!). There would be a great to do if one of us found our packet didn't have salt and we'd then have to beg for one of our pals to share their twist of salt…sometimes we'd open a packet and find two salts in it, that was like Christmas!

Even better was when we got home, Mum would usually have eggs and chips waiting for us (the eggs were deep-fried with the chips, smashing!) and what's more, there would be no vegetables!!!

The other thing we enjoyed about our visit to the baths was getting 'free' Brylcream for our hair as we left the pool. When I say 'free', it wasn't really; the baths had a coin machine which for a penny or two would dispense a 'blob' of hair cream into your hands which you then used on your hair, however, my pals and I would get ours 'free' by putting our mouths to the opening of the machine and sucking! This would get us enough Brylcream for our hair! This trick came in quite handy as we grew older and started taking a greater interest in the fairer sex!

Dad's work at the community centre kept him away from home for long hours (he was required to work a 48 hour week over six days, but the nature of his work saw him doing many hours more), and as the centre was only a couple of minutes' walk from our house, Dad would often get caught up in projects that would eat into his own time. Because of this, the centre became a large part of our lives too and I'd often be 'called in' by Dad to help with such chores as running off information sheets on the gestetner copier (we didn't have photocopy machines back then), then folding and distributing these throughout the district.

Through his work and his interest in people, Dad joined the World Friendship Association, which among other things saw Dad bringing all types of people, who visited the centre, home (at short notice) either for a meal or to stay for a few days. Mum never knew when to expect 'visitors' and it drove her 'mad' on occasions!

The first 'guests' that I recall were two Indian university students who were studying social work at Glasgow University; they were interested in the type of community work Dad was doing at the centre.

They were very 'proper' and their English was more English than the English! They were always picking me up about the way I spoke! One of the students, Shreekant, maintained contact with Mum and Dad for many years and we met with him in Colombo years later when we migrated to Australia.

Another guest was a young German student named Wolfgang with whom I became quite friendly, his attitude was much different from that of our two Indian guests.

Wolfgang was an avid stamp collector and among his luggage, he had a suitcase full of stamps from all over the world. On learning that I collected stamps, he spent some hours with me sorting through my collection and setting them out properly. Wolfgang gave me a selection of quite rare British stamps which would have been of value now if I had not 'lost' my stamp albums in our move to Australia!

Wolfgang was also very good at sketching and when he left I asked him to sign my autograph book and draw a flag with the swastika on it. I was too young to understand the abhorrence this symbol had with the German people and it was quite an awkward incident for Wolfgang, however, he handled the situation well in explaining to me my faux pas and I apologised to my friend for my indiscretion.

From France came Didier who was closer to my age and we, along with my cousin Leslie, did many things together in the time he spent with us in Glasgow.

On one occasion, the three of us cycled to Balmaha on Loch Lomond side and hired a rowing boat. We decided to row to one of the largest islands on the loch, Inchcailloch, to explore it. Didier was rowing the boat, and as we neared the edge of the island but was heading for a partly submerged log. Leslie and I frantically waved our arms and cried out in our best schoolboy French, "Gauche!" and "Droit!" for Didier to change direction, but our schoolboy French was clearly not understood and we ran aground! It took us quite some time to get our boat free and needless to say we didn't let Didier row again!

Didier corresponded with us from his home in Lyons for some years, but eventually, his contact was lost when my family moved to Australia.

Another initiative of Dad's that grew out of the Friendship Society was that of exchange visits with groups from Europe. In '53, the first exchange group to visit was the Danish Girls Choir, from Copenhagen. This group of girls and their leaders were billeted with families associated with the community centre. Their visit was written up in the *Glasgow Evening Citizen* newspaper as this was a first in this type of exchange, also it didn't do any harm that the girls were all so photogenic, being tall and blond with good figures!

Dad organised outings for the choir to different tourism areas of the countryside as well as involving them in singing engagements. The success of this first exchange visit paved the way for this to become an ongoing project. As usual, I managed to find my way into trouble, as these nice (innocent) Danish girls taught me a few words of Danish…unfortunately (unbeknown to me) they were swear words! Of course, being all of ten years old at this time, I had to show off what I'd learned and mouthed off the words at an official function…well, you can imagine what happened…

In later years, we had a group of Dutch girls stay with us and I was more of an age to appreciate the opposite sex. I had quite a crush on one of the girls, Annie, who, although a few years older than me, returned my interest and we developed quite a relationship. The following year when Dad organised an exchange visit to Holland, I met up with Annie and her family.

Annie and I would create quite a scene when she would 'double' me on her bicycle through her village, with me sitting 'side saddle' in my kilt! (Dad would often encourage those in our group to wear our national dress when on these exchange visits as a way of promoting Scotland.) Unfortunately, the distance was the 'curse' of such a romance and after a few months of exchanging letter, the relationship faded…

Still, I had a great time in Holland as I stayed with a family called the Jostens in a small village named Wijk aan Zee in Beverwik, and I became good pals with their son, Bob Josten, who was about my age and was an upcoming tennis player in the Netherlands. In the following year, Bob spent his holiday with me in Scotland. Bob was an instant hit with the girls, not only because of his good looks and tennis ability but also because of his Dutch accent when he spoke English; my pals and I benefited from this, of course!

I think that these exchange visits along with the different people that Dad would bring to our house helped give me a greater understanding of people from other countries as well as their cultures and it is something that has stood me in good stead throughout my life. Dad would often say to us, "We're all Jock Tamson's bairns," when explaining why we should appreciate other people and their cultures – I think it's a quote of Robert Burns…

Because of Dad's involvement with his work at the centre and his keenness to create new projects and programmes, he would often involve the family in these activities (whether we wanted to or not!). Such a case in point was when a Junior Orchestra commenced at the centre. Dad felt that we should all have the opportunity to gain an appreciation of music and all of us kids were involved in the orchestra at some stage, me first being the oldest.

In those days any boy learning an instrument (apart from the guitar or drums) was considered a 'sissy', so imagine my horror at having to join an orchestra! Dad bought me a violin and I was sent to lessons. I did everything in my power to get out of playing the violin; I'd miss lessons, forget to practice or leave my bow behind, anything to get out of playing! (and it cost me dearly in loss of pocket money and/or cuffs around the ears!).

In the end, Dad saw that the violin was a lost cause with me and he relented, but only as much as I had to choose another instrument…

I suggested the cello, as I thought Dad wouldn't be able to afford such, as it was a large and expensive piece of instrument…I was wrong! Somehow Dad found a cello for me and I was still in the orchestra. (Not that those in the orchestra particularly wanted me, as they could see I was no good!) I did my best to get out of playing the cello; on one occasion I let it fall off a train and it smashed to pieces (or so I thought!), but Dad did an amazing job of glueing it back together (I forgot his dad was a carpenter!) and I remained in the orchestra!

Not that the orchestra didn't have some good points, mainly girls! And over the years we had some great fun on weekends away and at parties.

Dad I'm sure, was way before his time as Glasgow didn't become the City of Culture till '90, yet in the '50s he had me not only in an orchestra but also in a boys' choir and a pipe band! He had also established 'eisteddfods' and many other cultural events with the Robert Burns Night, one of the most popular.

I didn't mind the Knightswood Boys Choir so much as a few of my pals from school were in it and our conductor, Mr Rennie, had a good understanding of boys and could bring out the best in us. He would always ensure that our repertoire contained a number of rousing songs that went down well with all the lads. The highlight of my time with the choir was when we sang in St. Andrew's Hall in Glasgow.

The Knightswood Pipe Band was where I learned to play the bagpipes, though unlike my father, I was never good at it. I think Dad enrolled me in the band because of my father being a piper and he felt I should have the opportunity to carry on the tradition. I persevered with piping, practising with the chanter twice a week (which at least kept me from practising the cello!) and graduating to the pipes, though I only played with the band a couple of occasions. The band went on to win a number of championships after I left for Australia!.

The band had a female Scottish country dance group attached to it, which was one of the attractions of the band and we had many good times going on trips and holidays as a group. My first real girlfriend was one of the country dancers, which was a great incentive for me to stay with the band!

In late '52, Dad bought our first television set, I think we were one of the first in the street to have one and my pals were always coming over to watch

'The Lone Ranger' or *'The Cisco Kid'* on a little black and white screen. The television was set in a wooden cabinet with doors that closed over the screen; it was a very handsome piece of furniture.

I can remember hurrying home from primary school to watch shows like *'Andy Pandy'* and *'Sooty'* as well as *'The Flowerpot Men'*. I was taken in by a young Australian cartoonist, Rolf Harris, who told stories about a little Aboriginal boy called 'Tumbarumba'. When we migrated to Australia, I was amazed to find there was a place named Tumbarumba which I visited in later years.

At night television had such shows as *'Animal, Vegetable Or Mineral?'* and *'This is Your Life'*, the latter which Eamonn Andrews made popular throughout the world. There were also 'thriller' serials such as *'The Little Red Monkey'* and *'The Quatermass Experiment'* which I used to watch through a crack in the living room door, as these were considered too frightening for youngsters…and they were! I'd sometimes sneak upstairs to bed having watched part of the show and stay awake for hours scared some monster might get me!

The biggest event on television happened in '53 – the coronation of Queen Elizabeth II. While the Queen and the Royal family were highly regarded by the majority of the Scottish people, it was a sore point with the Scottish nationalists that the Queen was crowned Queen Elizabeth II as the previous Queen Elizabeth (known as the Virgin Queen) had reigned prior to the union of the crowns, thus she was Elizabeth of England only. Minor protests saw buildings and pillar-boxes with the EIIR on them vandalised in Glasgow (some pillar boxes were actually blown up!).

Dad went to a lot of trouble setting up our living room with tiered benches so that we could squeeze in all our relatives, friends and neighbours. We had over fifty adults squashed into the room and us kids had to sit or lie on the floor to watch the proceedings. We were all glued to the little screen for hours as Richard Dimbleby of the BBC talked us through the whole ceremony, from when the Queen left Buckingham Palace to the crowning at Westminster Abbey.

I recall that not long after her coronation, the Queen visited Glasgow and all us school children were taken to Scotstoun Showground to see her. The Queen and the Duke of Edinburgh passed within feet of us in an open Land Rover and we all broke ranks to chase their vehicle, cheering at the top of our voices.

Before television came along, evenings were spent around the wireless as families listened to their favourite shows or music programmes. *'The*

McFlannels' was very popular as it was a series about a Scottish family in Glasgow (it was a bit like *'The Broons'* in the *Sunday Post* newspaper). Another radio show we enjoyed was Wilfred Pickles's *'Ask Pickles'* which was an early talkback show where questions were asked and Wilfred had to find the answer, it was always good for a laugh.

As I entered my teens, however, 'Radio Luxemburg' took up most of my listening time as it played 'pop' and 'rock and roll' non-stop. Radio Luxemburg was broadcasted from a ship anchored in the English Channel, which allowed it to get around certain broadcasting regulations. I can remember listening to the music and wondering if 'rock and roll' would be 'dead' before I was old enough to be a part of it.

Dad also had a shortwave radio set which I'd often listen to as it could not only pick up programmes from around the world but also ships messages and conversations between 'ham' radio operators. Just listening to these voices opened up a whole new world for me.

In '51, the Empire Exhibition came to Glasgow and Dad took me along to it. I found it fascinating with so many unusual and interesting displays, however, the thing that caught my eye most was a gyroscope, which was something I'd never seen before and it held me spellbound as it maintained its balance on a wire strung between two poles…this gave me another item for my Christmas 'wish list'!

One of the saddest days for me in this era was when my Granma Winton died in '56; she was sixty-six years old. It was the first funeral I attended and I remember sitting on my Papa Winton's knees, in his home in Denniston, feeling very sad and watching with apprehension at those present sipped cups of tea and gave their condolences to Papa.

Later that day Papa's sister, Aunt Hana, and her husband, Uncle Tommy, gave me two figurines of elephants (these were black with white ivory tusks), I think mainly to help me get over the sadness of the day. They had brought these back from the African Gold Coast on one of their many visits to that continent. Uncle Tommy was a saw doctor and did a lot of overseas travel.

Between my schooldays, pals and family, my years were full ones until in '57 we moved again to Kinellar Drive which was about two miles from where we lived. Our new home was larger and as well as having up and down stairs, we had a front and back yard to ourselves!…and with a railway line at the bottom of our garden who needed fairies!

Christmas Was for Kids!!!

Christmas was always a magical time when I was little; even more so when it was a 'white' one. Christmas was for kids and there was an air of excitement as the days grew shorter and the nights got colder and there was frost on the ground.

We believed in Santa till a much older age. I think I was nearly into my tenth year before I understood what he was all about…I still believe in Santa and think Christmas is the most magical time of all…

I recall that once school term finished, Mum would take me into town to the large retail shop called the 'Polytechnic' to visit Santa in his snow cave; though the memory is still vivid, I must have been very young at the time because neither my brother or sisters were with us.

The cave would have different scenes, sometimes of nursery rhymes or sometimes of elves and fairies that would be helping Santa put together his Christmas list. I was always on my best behaviour as I'd been warned that Santa wouldn't grant my wishes if I wasn't good…and I was never what you would call a 'good' child! But Christmas and Santa brought out the best in me! Children would be queued up in hundreds with stars in their eyes waiting to see Santa. It was a big part of the Christmas magic visiting Santa in his snow cave…

Preparations for Christmas would start months before as we gathered the necessary bits and pieces needed to make our Christmas decorations (most decorations were homemade – commercialism hadn't quite taken over as yet!). The main decorations were 'paper chains' which were made of different coloured paper and strung around the room; the other was milk bottle tops. Milk bottle tops were made of foil and came in three bright colours, red, blue and silver. These would be carefully prized off the milk bottle, washed then turned into decorations to hang off the Christmas tree.

At school we would make paper lanterns, some out of different coloured paper and some we would paint with designs; these would be hung with pride on our families Christmas tree.

Mum would have prepared her 'clootie' dumpling and her blackcurrant and ginger wine by late November, and these would be sitting in the cool darkness of the pantry quietly maturing for the festive season.

Christmas trees in those days were real and the scent of the pine needles sometimes with real candles carefully placed among the branches created the magic that was Christmas…fairy lights were still very basic in the '50s and quite expensive.

The postman would deliver parcels (from aunts and uncles) almost on a daily basis, and in those days we really had a postal service, the postie would come regularly twice a day and at Christmas time you could expect deliveries any time of the day even quite late on Christmas Eve!

From early December Mum would be hiding these parcels in the linen press or under beds or down in the 'glory hole'. These would be brought out and placed under the Christmas tree on Christmas Eve once all us kids were tucked safely in bed.

Before retiring to bed we'd all hang our school stockings up by the mantelpiece by the fire and leave a piece of cake and some milk for Santa (we always used our school stockings as these were the longest and could hold the most!).

While the fire was still burning, we would write a note to Santa telling him that we'd been good and asking him to leave us something special in our Christmas stocking (Mum and Dad always checked the note to see that what was being asked was not too high in expectations!). The notes would then be thrown onto the fire and we'd watch as our papers would burn and turn to ash then fly up the chimney where, we believed, they would be caught by Santa's fairies and taken to his workshop in the North Pole…this would ensure that Santa knew what we wished for…

On Christmas morning, our stockings would be full to overflowing with 'goodies'; there would be sweets, games, comic books, small toys, fruit and nuts and usually some money, while down at the very toe of the stocking would be a special present…that was where I got my first watch. Larger presents (which came from our relatives) were placed in bundles under the Christmas tree.

My earliest recollection of Christmas, apart from the one I spent in the hospital, was of when Santa brought me a large wooden aeroplane painted bright green with the royal air force markings on its wings. I also got a farmyard with all the animals made out of wood, my favourite of which was a black and white border collie which sat on its haunches and looked just like the real thing. Dad had made these toys, a skill he had learned in part from his father who was a master tradesman in carpentry; Dad was still making toys and dolls houses some thirty years later for his granddaughters!

My aeroplane, which was similar in shape to the 'Dakota' aircraft of that era, ran on wheels and was large enough for me to sit on and push myself around, and I used to ride down the footpath at Harefield Drive with my feet up on the wings…it was my favourite toy for many years.

When I was about eight years old Santa brought me my first two-wheeler bike for Christmas, it was bright red…I couldn't wait to show it off to my pals. It was one of those white Christmases with fresh snow on the ground, and as I peddled towards my pals I pulled on the brakes, skidded and went head over heels over the handlebars and into the snow! Lucky for me it was a soft landing! It was a rather crestfallen youngster who then showed off his new bike to his pals!

Mum's cousin, who I called Aunt Isa, lived not far from us in Knightswood and she would often hold a Christmas party for the relatives and their children. (Aunt Isa was a spinster so had no children of her own.) Her house was always the most beautifully decorated with the loveliest of Christmas trees in pride of place in the living room. Aunt Isa would have presents for all the children and would have one of the uncles dress up as Santa and give these out.

One year I got a 'spud gun' (a toy gun that shot bits of potato) from Santa…I was really excited as I'd never had a gun before (Dad never allowed us to have guns; he had been a conscientious objector during the war, refusing to take up arms and had served his time with a non-combatant company and then with the Quakers). Somehow during the evening festivities, my gun disappeared and I never saw it again…so I had to continue playing 'cowboys and Indians' with my pals using my fingers as my 'six-shooters'!

I remember one Christmas when both Alastair and I got white rabbits from Santa; I would have been about ten or eleven years old. These were beautiful animals with big pink eyes and soft fluffy white coats. Alistair's lived about three days, mine for about a week; I remember crying at night because our pets had died. I found it hard to understand that something so loveable could die so easily. This is the only time that I can recall some sadness over the Christmas period…

Over the years my cousin Leslie and I had developed a strong friendship (even though I was apt to be the aggressive one and could be somewhat of a bully to Leslie); we did many things together as we grew up. One Christmas when we were about twelve years old, we were invited to spend Christmas with Aunt May (Mum's elder sister) who lived in Manchester. Aunt May and her husband, Uncle Donald, lived in a large rambling old house with about eight bedrooms as well as a big old kitchen and a solarium in which Uncle Donald kept hundreds of cacti.

Uncle Donald had been a scientist during the war with the Royal Navy (among other things he helped perfect the sight on the Enfield rifle) and the house was full of electronic equipment, with which Leslie and I had great fun playing. Our favourite piece of machinery was a kind of gun turret, which had been used to train our spitfire pilots during the war. This large box-like piece of equipment (a bit like an early version of the video car games of today) had a black and white television screen built in it and you had to sit in an aeroplane's chair with headphones on and watch the screen.

There was a 'joystick' with a firing button on it, and when you lined up the cross on the screen with the target plane, you pressed the button and the screen recorded whether you hit or missed the target. A direct 'hit' would see the plane belch smoke and dive off the edge of the screen. Leslie and I would never get tired of playing with this piece of equipment.

Uncle Donald's connection with this side of the war saw him acquire a piece of the Messerschmitt plane which Rudolf Hess flew to Scotland to try to broker peace with the allies. This piece of equipment stood on his mantelpiece for many years.

When I visited Scotland in '90, Aunt May asked me if I might like this piece of memorabilia (Uncle Donald having passed away some years before), but I felt it should remain with my aunt while she was alive…I often wondered what happened to this piece of history when my aunt passed away a few years later…

Uncle Donald was also very keen on motorcars and had a beautiful old black jaguar with dual fuel tanks, which he'd often take us for a run in; and quite often he'd have to flick the switch over to the reserve fuel tank as he'd forgotten to fill up with petrol – part of the nature of being a scientist, I think!

He also had built a rather stunning sports car body out of fibreglass (I think), but under the bonnet was a Volkswagen engine, and Leslie and I were always surprised when 'ordinary' cars passed us, or we couldn't keep up with fast-moving vehicles!

At night we'd join our aunt and her friends and play canasta in front of a blazing log fire in the living room. Leslie and I became quite proficient at this game and my aunt's friends said they'd give us a set of canasta cards each to encourage us to keep playing…Leslie received his but somehow I never got mine…But, we had great fun on that Christmas holiday, it was the first time we had been away on our own and we felt very grown-up.

It was the year that the song *'Gilly Gilly Ossenfeffer Katzenellenbogan by the Sea'* was popular. Leslie and I would sing it together, often arguing about who should lead and who should repeat the chorus! But my aunt and her friends made a great fuss of our singing and would often ask for an encore! That year, it was a white Christmas which made Manchester look like something out of a Dickens novel…until the fogs set in!

Fogs in Manchester in the '50s were real 'pea-soupers', and I recall one night returning home from town with the bus driver being shown the road by the conductor walking in front of the bus, shining his torch on the kerbside to show the way!

It was not much different in Glasgow during winter, as it too could have really bad fog being such an industrial city…and with everyone burning coal in their fires in winter, this only added to the problem. The compensation for us kids was that most winters we had snow and we'd spend most evenings out with our pals sledging on the hills in the parks around the neighbourhood or skating (or sliding) on the ponds.

There was a small pond near Knightswood Park, which would sometimes freeze over in winter, and when we were tired of sledging we'd often make our way to this pond and play sliding on the ice. There was an old man at the pond who sold hot chestnuts and for a penny or two, we'd get enough hot chestnuts to eat and keep us warm as we headed home.

Walking home at night from our sledging or ice skating was never boring as almost every house in every street we walked along had a Christmas tree in the window with coloured lights that twinkled at us through the frost. Sometimes we'd be late getting home and our parents would scold us because they thought we might have come to harm, and we'd always say, "But Mum, you should've seen the fairy lights on the trees…we didn't realise it was so late…" and usually we'd be forgiven on the promise that we'd watch our time in future…but we never did!

Of course George Square, in the centre of the city was where the best display of Christmas lights and decorations were. The whole square would be ablaze with lights and right in the centre would be the tallest Christmas tree you'd ever see. This tree came as a gift each year from the citizens of Norway as a 'thank you' for what the British had done for them during World War II. It was always one of our favourite treats to be taken into the city to see George Square…and then maybe have a visit to the Kelvin Hall.

The Kelvin Hall was a beautiful old Victorian building of red sandstone which stood opposite the Glasgow Art Gallery in the suburb of Kelvingrove. At Christmas time, the circus would come to town and the 'big tent' would be set up inside the Kelvin Hall along with the sideshows and funfair.

Circuses in those days were the real thing, with lots of wild animals on display doing all sorts of tricks, from dancing bears to lions and tigers performing acrobatics in the same ring. It was usually a 'three-ring' circus and there would be activities simultaneously in all rings; wild animals in one, clowns in another and the trapeze artists in the third…it was a great treat at Christmas to go to the circus…and afterwards spend time in the sideshows.

The favourite of all the rides in the sideshow 'alley' was the 'helter-skelter', which was a slide whose top reached the roof of the Kelvin Hall and its slide spiralled all the way down to the ground. You rode down on hessian sacks (old potato bags, I think!) at an amazing speed. It was always the highlight of the outing. (I was most disappointed when I visited Glasgow in '90 to find that the 'helter-skelter' was no more and the Kelvin Hall had been turned into a sporting venue.)

The other treat at this time of year was to go to the 'pantomimes', these were great fun for all the family, and us kids would be out of our seats booing the baddies and cheering for the goodies in productions such as *'Babes in the Woods'*, *'Cinderella'* or *'Dick Whittington'*. In pantomimes, the leading 'man' was always a woman, while in shows like *'Cinderella'* the ugly sisters were men and us kids would almost fall out of our seats laughing at their antics. A night out at the pantomime would keep us in stories for weeks afterwards.

Of course, it wouldn't be Christmas if there weren't a gathering of all the relatives at sometime over the holiday period. Usually, on Boxing Day we'd all go to Dad's parent's place (Granma & Granpa Waddell) at Carntyne. We'd catch the tram or trolleybus to their place which would take about an hour or so as they lived on the East side of Glasgow. We always enjoyed going to Granma

Waddell's place as she was our favorite among the grandparents, mainly because she never played favorites and always had time for each one of us.

We were allowed quite a bit of freedom under the 'protection' of Granma (like, I'd never have to eat my vegetables!) and we'd enjoy the time playing with our cousins and opening up our Christmas presents that Santa had somehow left at Gran's for us!

Christmas dinners were a real treat too; the chicken was still somewhat of a luxury, and to have roast chicken at Christmas was something to look forward to…as well, the vegetables were usually roast potatoes and peas – something I could handle! But the sweets were the best! Trifles and steaming hot plum pudding with custard as well as a 'clootie' dumpling which was a must. And if you weren't lucky enough to find a silver threepenny bit in your piece of plum pudding, you could be sure Granma would find one in your bit of dumpling!…us kids never went home without money in our pockets!

I loved the Christmas season and just couldn't wait for it to come around each year; it was such a magical time when I was growing up…there was only one drawback, however. As I was born on the twelfth day of Christmas (5 January), often, when I was a little older, I would be given a present from an aunt or uncle with the comment "Merry Christmas!…and this is for your birthday too…" As I really loved getting presents, it was always a bit of a disappointment to have Christmas and birthday presents rolled into one…

New Year, or Hogmanay as it is known in Scotland (Hogmanay is the last day of the year), was the biggest celebration of the year for adults, much more so than Christmas, but it held little for the children – though there was a custom that a gift was given to children who asked for one on New Year's Eve; this was most likely to pacify the youngsters so the adults could go out 'first-footing'. The first-footing was a major event in Glasgow; it was considered good luck if your 'first-foot' for the New Year was a dark-haired man. As Dad was dark-haired, he and Mum would go off into the early hours of the morning 'first-footing' all their friends, usually with a piece of coal in one pocket (to ensure that those visited would have warmth throughout the year) and a bottle of whisky in the other! They used to have a grand time at 'Ne'erday' and found it something of a let-down when we emigrated to Australia where New Year celebrations were almost non-existent in the '50s.

*Photo taken in 1930s of the Winton/Marshall
families at West Kilbride.
David and Anna are on the left of
the 2nd row*

Mum aged 14, with David Winton in 1931

Best pals, Dave Waddell and David Winton 1932

*my mother with her
mother (Gran Marshall) in 1937*

Dave & David near Loch Lomond 1938

*David Winton at Harrow Weald
Park mansion in 1938 where he was
studying to be a lay preacher*

*'Uncle Dave' (on right) with his mother
(Gran Waddell) and brother Roy in 1939*

*My granma & Papa Winton at
Rothsey in the late 1940s.*

Mrs & Mrs David Winton – My parent's wedding 1940

38 Harefield Drive Scotston
where I was born on 5th January 1943

My uncle Jack (Winton) with me on my Christening day.
He was to die in a plane crash in Canada three months after my father's death.

With mum and 'Uncle Dave'
on the shores of Loch Lomond 1944

After my father's death, 'Uncle Dave' regularly sent me postcards from war torn
Europe.
These cards were produced by the American Armed Forces network featuring the
adventures of G.I Joe.

Mum & Me - July 1943

with mum and her twin sister Ruby and my cousin, Leslie in the front garden of Harefield Drive 1943. My papa Marshall is sitting in the background smoking a pipe

With Papa Winton Rothsey 1944

'Uncle Dave' and me at the seaside 1946

Mr. & Mrs. Waddell's marriage 1946
...and 'uncle Dave' becomes 'Dad'!

Mum & me at Fintry Baths,
just north of Glasgow 1946

me with my mum and 'new' Dad 1946

On my wheelbarrow 1946

With my baby brother, Alastair July '46

Whiteinch Park 1947

Granma Marshall with her four grandkids 1948
Leslie, Jim. Alastair and me in the front garden at Harefield drive, Scotstoun

Scotstoun Primary School 1948
I am at top left of photo

1949 our caravan at the Lake District
where I learned to swim

*Alastair and me looking down on
the Village of Port Appin 1950*

*Our 'But 'n' Ben at Port Appin with Dad's sister(Aunt Betty) and her two daughters,
Helen & Marion, as well as Gran Waddell, with Papa Waddell asleep in a deckchair
outside the front door.*

*Gran & papa Waddell at Port
Appin with their grandkids 1950*

Mum with Lana and Alastair and me on Loch Linnie 1950

Fiona, me, Lana and Alastair Christmas 1951

Dad and me at Pollock Community Centre,
where Dad was warden 1951

On the sands at Carnoustie 1952

Alastair & me on the Campsie Fells in
Winter with our 'jeely pieces' 1952

Family holiday at Billowness 1953

High School – Long Pants, Baggy Knees and The Strap

In July '55, I graduated to Victoria Drive Senior Secondary School – I only made the grade by the skin of my teeth, getting a J1 pass (the lowest possible to get into a senior secondary school). I can remember Mum giving me a great hug when I told her I'd got into senior secondary school – she wasn't so impressed when she found out that I only scraped in! Mum was very aware that my cousin Leslie was a good scholar and didn't like the thought of me not matching him (which I never did!).

Victoria Drive Senior Secondary School (we always had to stress the 'senior' secondary as 'junior' secondary schools were tailored towards trades and 'non-professional' careers) was to play a major part in my life over the next few years…Scholastically though, I'm not sure that it had a great impact! I was always something of a 'daydreamer' and secondary school didn't quite fit my psyche. Often, I would be unsure of what class I was meant to be at or in which building…but overall my time and my pals at Victoria Drive was a positive experience.

The school had two main compounds, which were about half a mile from one and other; the main building was a beautiful old building of Victorian design in the red sandstone which was common in Glasgow, while the other was more of a temporary structure and housed the woodwork and metalwork rooms in addition to a few classrooms. Our playing fields were at Scotstoun Showground's, about two miles away, close to Whiteinch Park.

(I was aghast when I visited Scotland in 2002 to find that there was nothing left of the main building except the perimeter fence and the stonework at the entrance to the 'boys' gate!)

Our high school also separated the boys from the girls in the classrooms and in the playgrounds of the main complex (it was not possible to do this in the temporary complex) and this was strictly enforced; any boy caught in the girl's area would be up for a few strokes of the strap (I cannot remember such punishment being meted out to girls). The 'janie' (the school janitor) would take great delight in reporting any boy who broke the rules…was it any wonder we all 'hated' the janie!

The first six months high school was a real learning experience for me; primary school had never been much of a problem as far as study was concerned, but all of a sudden we were into 'education'! French, maths, science… it was all Greek to me! While I could hold my own in the arts, I could never get my head around these other subjects…and my report card showed this!

Us 'new kids' ('preps' as we were called) were quite intimidated by the 'big boys' and prefects of the school and for the first year we kept a low profile; we were all pleased when we made it into second year and had 'new kids' under us, we were no longer the bottom of the heap!

Secondary school was when we also 'graduated' to long pants (it was short pants summer and winter for us boys before this). Our school uniform was grey flannel trousers and a dark blue blazer; it took us some time to get used to wearing our 'flannels' as, if you didn't pull your pants up at the knees before you sat down you ended up with trousers that were baggy at the knees…you could always tell the boys who had just graduated from short pants because of their baggy knees.

Dad, who was always on the lookout for bargains in school clothing, took me to 'Hoyles', a menswear shop in Partick, where he had spied a boy's suit on sale…and unfortunately (for me) it was just my size, so Dad snapped it up. This suit was to be the bane of my life while it lasted, it was a heavy tweed material of a light grey/blue base, with a blue and white check pattern running through it. I stood out like a 'sore toe' at school and was always getting into scraps as my pals would call me a 'poof', or worse! Luckily for me, the suit didn't last long (I'm sure the fights I had while wearing it helped its demise!).

Dad also did the 'running' repairs on our school shoes (as did many of the other kids' Dads of this era). He would replace the soles of our shoes with leather, which he would cut to shape, then to get longer wear out of them he'd nail cleats to the toes and heels (which made them great for sliding on ice in the wintertime!) But despite all Dads' efforts I still managed to go through a pair of shoes in no time at all.

Morning and afternoon breaks were the most enjoyable times of the school day as we'd all get our pals together and play 'fitba'. At any time during these breaks, you could find 'fitba' games going on all over the playground and heaven help anyone who got in the road!

We had quite a large number of boys from the new housing estate of Drumchapel in our year (they had been relocated from areas such as Partick and Whiteinch under the Glasgow Corporation's housing scheme). These lads saw themselves as a wee bit different from those of us who lived nearer the school (and what's more they were all pretty good at footy) and while we were all pals overall when it came to playground football, it was always the 'scruffs' against the 'poofs'!

These games, played on an asphalt surface with a tennis ball were a matter of life and death as we fought for supremacy; sometimes we were so engrossed in our game we wouldn't hear the period bell ring!

The playground was also the place where we 'sorted one and other out' and there would be hardly a day go by but there wasn't some kind of scuffle or fight; most forgotten five minutes after the incident. In my time, I was involved in my share and mostly gave as good as I got, though I never perfected the 'Glasgow kiss' (Gie'm the heid Jimmy!) unlike some. My pal Hamish came off the worst for wear from one such head butt delivered in the boy's urinal…brought tears to his eyes, but he was over it in a few minutes…and much the wiser in playground fights!

In the classroom it was a different matter, strong discipline was enforced and if any boy (or girl for that matter) was seen to be out of line, then the 'belt' came out! The belt (or 'strap' as it was sometimes called) was a piece of leather about quarter inch thick and two feet in length with three 'tails' at one end…and all teachers used it, some better than others! There would hardly be a lesson where the 'belt' didn't come into play…some of us got it regularly (myself among those I must admit).

You could be given the 'belt' for any number of reasons such as not doing homework, talking in class, giving a wrong answer, disrupting the class, coming late to class, sitting in the wrong seat in the classroom or just seeming to be annoying to the teacher!

But the majority of our teachers were pretty even handed, (I don't mean they could use the belt in both hands!); they could see our sense of humour on occasions. I recall one morning when our teacher was doing 'role call' and he called out the name, "Brian McCoo!". Brian happened to be off sick that day and when the teacher asked where's McCoo, one of the 'lads' called out, "He's havin' a wee calf" (Week off) ! Very droll the teacher replied, "I only wish you could be as smart at your lessons!"

The 'jannie' (the school's janitor) could also get you a 'belting' as he'd report you for misdemeanours in the playground. The 'jannie' always seemed to be spying on us lads and he was one person we loved to hate!

I once got a 'belting' for smiling in class and I didn't even realise I was smiling! First thing I knew was when the teacher said, "Winton! Take that smile off your face!"

"What smile Sir? I'm not smiling."

"Winton, that's insolence! Come out here!"…and I got six of the best! (six belts with the strap was the maximum allowed on one hand).

But I wasn't the only one who would get the strap for nothing (in our opinion). One lad in our class, John Elder, just couldn't help himself, he'd get the strap almost every lesson, so much that he wrote a poem about his predicament and it was published in the school magazine!

John's poem was called 'Ecstasy'…

'It was so weird and wonderful,
I can't say how it felt,
That day, the one and only,
I didn't have the belt.
The teachers cheered, the boys all gazed
The girls began to scream;
Then suddenly I nipped myself
And found it was a dream.'

which only goes to show that there is more to a person than meets the eye.

John, in having his verse published in the school magazine accomplished something which I never did, despite entering articles every year. It was something I always felt disappointed about, similar to my never being chosen to take part in the Christmas pageants in primary school.

John, or Elder as he was usually called (we were all called by our second names or a nickname), was by far the biggest boy in our class, he was a bit of a loner, not being into sport much nor academically minded (like many of us!) and he could be a bully at times. While Elder was on the fringe of our group, the 'lads' would always be having a 'dig' at him and heaven help you if he heard you or found out about it!

One incident with Elder will remain with me for as long as I live; it kind of reflects the way things were in the '50s, especially in regards to discipline. We were in our English class waiting for our teacher, Mr Sieth, to arrive and we were all getting a bit restless. One of our gang, Jimmy (who was about the smallest in the class, but full of the cheek) made a smart remark to Elder and Elder went for him! I thought Jimmy was in for a hiding, so I gave my glasses to one of my pals (I'd learned by this time to take my glasses off before getting into a fight!) and dived on Elder. He turned on me and Jimmy scarpered!

Elder and I were locked together fighting (well, he was fighting, I was holding on for grim death!) we were rolling around under the desks when the teacher came in; we were so engrossed in our scuffle that we didn't hear the class go quiet. Mr Sieth roared, "Winton! Elder! What are you doing?" We broke up immediately and it was no good giving our usual answer of "Nothing, Sir!"

Mr Sieth called us out to the front of the class and asked us what we were fighting for, then without waiting for a reply said that no one fought in his classroom and gave us both twelve lashes with the strap (maximum punishment) then sent us back to our seats. Jimmy had got off 'scot-free'! Our fingers were so swollen that for the next two periods neither of us could hold a pen and I had to walk home at lunchtime as I couldn't close my hands around my bike's handlebars!

Worst was to come. When I complained to Dad about the injustice of being belted for trying to protect my pal, Dad gave me a 'cuff on the lug' for causing trouble at school! How things have changed!

Following this incident, the news spread like wildfire around the school that Elder and Winton had had a scuffle in class and it was going to be sorted out after school. At the afternoon play break, Elder approached me in the playground and asked if I wanted to go on with it after school to which I replied it was up to him but I wasn't backing down…After a bit of huffing and puffing and eyeing one and other, Elder extended his hand to me and we shook hands (I can tell you it was more than my hands that were shaking at the time!). So the fight was off; Elder and I made up and from then on while not quite becoming the best of pals, we had a grudging respect for one and other.

Mr Sieth was something of an 'idol' with the boys as he was one of the teachers who could really wield the belt. He stood no-nonsense but was always seen as fair in his punishments. One of his 'tricks' which gave him respect was his ability while writing on the blackboard, to hear you talking or causing disruption and be able to turn and hurl his piece of chalk at you with unerring accuracy. If you were lucky enough the chalk bouncing off your head was considered enough punishment…unless you were foolish enough to disrupt the class again!

Another incident I had with Mr Sieth was when I was about to be punished for something; I can't remember what the punishment was for – there were so many of them! He asked me if I knew our school motto. Thinking it might save me a belting I said, "It's something written in Latin above the 'Head's door'" (stupid answer!) Mr Sieth then interpreted the Latin for me (and the class) while giving me a belt with the strap for every line in the stanza…I still can't remember the motto, but it went something like this:

'Because of the nail, (whack!) the shoe was lost, (whack!)
    because of the shoe (whack!) the horse was lost, (whack!)
Because of the horse (whack!) the rider was lost, (whack!)
    because of the rider, the battle was lost…'
…somehow I missed the point…

Beltings were something of a badge of honour with the boys, and sometimes we'd go out of our way to get 'the strap' with teachers who couldn't hurt you with the leather. It was considered cowardly if you drew your hand(s) away so that the strap missed you (though this usually meant you got an extra belt added…or in Mr Sieth's case, two!).

However, in the second year, we had a couple of quite pretty female teachers who were not so proficient with the strap. The boys often used to draw their hands away at the last moment and the strap would catch the female teacher's skirt and sometimes reveal a bit of thigh…which would bring wolf whistles from the class! Our French teacher, Miss Axeworthy, put a stop to this when she sent any boy, who withdrew his hands, to Mr Sieth for punishment!

Despite this 'corporal punishment' I never felt that any of our teachers were malevolent or sadistic towards us pupils, something that was often quoted by Catholic or private school pupils in 'letter to the editor' in latter years.

Miss Axeworthy was considered by all the boys to be the prettiest in the school, as I remember, she was petite with a nice figure…her French accent most likely helped too. (None of which, however, helped us in the learning of our French!)

We were at the stage where we had started to take more than an interest in the opposite sex and some of the gamer lads in the French class would, on a dare from a pal, deliberately bump into Miss Axeworthy just to boast that they had 'touched' her body! I'm not sure whether the teacher was ever aware of this 'game' among the boys, but one time it backfired on me and I wasn't even being dared! It happened as I was talking with my pals and walking backwards along the corridor between classrooms, and I accidentally bumped into Miss Axeworthy. She yelled at me asking what I was doing not looking where I was going, I went bright red! My pals got a laugh out of me for weeks after the incident! (and I as usual got the belt!)

In my second year at Victoria Drive, I was in Class 11F (down a grade from the first year). This class was mainly made up of the boys who were not so academically inclined…or were disinterested in the concept of study! It wasn't that we weren't bright, just our interests were elsewhere, as our music teacher would say of us, we were stupid but saveable!

Our music teacher was a Miss Symes (all female teachers were 'Miss' in those days) and she tried so hard to make something out of us musically. We did have one or two boys in the class who could hold a tune but the rest of us were a disaster. Miss Symes would have us practising our vowels for days on end, but when it came to singing we'd be like a cat's concert. We could manage the simple tunes like *'Nut Brown Maiden'* or *'Marie's Wedding'* but anything more difficult or the singing of 'rounds' would see us to convulse into hysterics, as we forgot the lines or what place we were at…which usually ended up with some of us getting belted!

Some of her lessons did rub off, however, as when I joined the Knightswood Boys Choir in later years. I always remembered her saying "Pronounce your vowels properly, shape your mouth to the sound and always finish your words by pronouncing the last consonant of the word…as in silent night…not nigh…" So I did learn something!

By the end of my second year at Victoria Drive, I had given up on French (the incident with the Miss Axeworthy aside) and had taken up the more practical subjects of woodwork and metalwork, which I found more to my liking and was reasonably good at. Science, which was a compulsory subject, was mainly of interest because of the mercury that we could steal or cause havoc with the Bunsen burners!

However, even in classes I enjoyed, I could still get into trouble. One woodwork lesson we were practising making 'dovetail' joints and the teacher had just warned us about being careful in the way we used the chisel. He'd no sooner spoken then my chisel slipped and went into my left hand just below my thumb. I saw spots before my eyes and almost fainted. The teacher gave me first aid…then six of the best for being careless! (I still have a small scar on my hand today, where the chisel cut me.)

Maths was also the bane of my life and unlike French, you could not drop the subject. It didn't help matters that in our third year, which was the Leaving Certificate year, we had several maths teachers! That year, I really outdid myself only scoring eighteen marks out of a possible one hundred! I still have my report card from that period, and my daughters take great delight in reminding me of my failures! (I could never come to grip with 'the square of the hypotenuse being equal to the square of the other two sides' or as one of our math's teachers so rightly called it 'the bridge of asses'…and I was one!)

Luckily, I scored well in all my other subjects, coming second in the class…but maths, ugh! A disaster! I never remember doing much homework, which was most likely a major contributor to my downfall in this subject. When it came to answering questions in class, especially the maths classes, I was one of the ones who seldom knew the answers (most likely because I seldom did the homework!).

However, there was a way around this. Rather than sitting there looking sheepish and waiting for the teacher to 'pounce' on you, we'd join with the rest of the class, waving our hand in the air and shouting "Sir! Sir! Me Sir!" (or Miss as the case may be) Of course if we were asked and didn't know the answer, we got the belt just the same, but the odds seemed more in our favour if we joined in the shouting!

Some periods we'd have teachers who'd set us an assignment or reading to do in class and then leave us to it. That was a disaster for the ones who had a short concentration span or were just bored by the subject…which was quite a few of us! In these situations, we would end up playing cards or reading comics under our desks while attempting to look studious! And we didn't get caught that much, but when we did, 'whamo!' six of the best!

My favourite subject was 'art'. I was quite good at drawing and I looked forward to the periods when our class would catch a tram to the Glasgow Art Gallery for art appreciation.

One year, I was picked along with my pal Sandy Allen (who was the best artist in our class) and a few others to enter a painting competition, run by Cadburys Chocolates. It had entrants from schools all over Scotland, and I got the greatest thrill when I received a 'treasure chest' of chocolates from Cadburys, as my work won a minor prize.

I was always drawing 'Disney' characters, which I'd been doing from an early age, and I at one time entertained the thought of becoming a commercial artist and perhaps working for the Disney Studios, but like most early ideas, it faded with time. Sandy, on the other hand, would draw these amazingly intricate drawings of space ships and planets. I don't know if he followed this talent of his but I'm sure he would have been a great asset to those on the 'Star Wars' films.

School sports were more to my liking and I usually made the athletic team for my class along with my pal Hamish . We were both pretty fast, but when it came to the school carnival, we could never beat the boys in the class above us in the four hundred yards relay, no matter how hard we tried.

I also played for the school rugby team on occasions, and I remember one 'away' game where we had to chase the cows off the field before we could play! My claim to fame on this day was stopping my opposite winger from scoring a try and both of us ending up with cow dung all over us…he wasn't impressed! It was one time I really enjoyed the showers and 'plunge' pool after the game!

Swimming was another sport that was encouraged at Victoria Drive and part of this activity was the attainment of the Royal Lifesaving bronze medallion. Once a week we'd take the tram to Whiteinch baths where we would practice our lifesaving. At the end of the semester, we all attained our bronze medallion award; many then went on to gain their bar to the bronze in following semesters.

Usually, swimming was the last period of the day and when it finished my pals and I would often stay on at the baths and play 'tag' in the pool or practice our diving off the diving dale…or when the pool attendant wasn't watching we'd 'bomb' the swimmers from this platform (which was about fifteen feet high)…if we were caught we were thrown out! (but at least we couldn't be belted!)

We would practice all sorts of dives from the diving dale and many of my pals became very good at these, Sandy Allan in particular, he could do handstands, back dives and somersaults with ease. We would also have competitions to see how far we could swim underwater, and many of us could complete two lengths of the pool (seventy-five yards each way) with a dive off the diving dale.

The reason this complex was called 'baths' was because not only did it have a swimming pool, it also had steam baths and Turkish baths as well as a pool exclusively for the women.

My sporting activities came to an end when I contracted eczema in my early teens. (I'd always had sensitive skin and this skin disease really got a hold on me, so much so that I was actually hospitalised at one stage while trying to bring it under control.) While I tried to keep up my sport (swimming was out of the question), the eczema was so bad that if I tried to run my skin would just crack open. My legs especially were terrible with this disease and I'd often have to go to school with them painted with a tar formula and wrapped in bandages… I was something of an oddity at school (like the two-headed man at the circus!) when like this and I not only drew strange looks but some name calling as well…another reason I got into scraps!

However, despite all of this I had some good pals at school and we'd go around in a kind of loose gang and getting into our share of mischief…One of our pals, Brian (Houston), whom I had known since primary school, would often bring rather sexually explicit photos to school for us to 'gawk' over (His dad was a professional photographer who was producing these for a sex manual.)We'd often be sitting up the back of the classroom passing these photos around under the desks – no wonder our lessons suffered! But I guess these were really where I got my sex education from…we definitely didn't get any from our parents in those days! I don't recall any of us ever being caught with these photos nor did Brian ever seem to get found out when he 'pinched' these from his dad!

Of course, 'sex' was a major interest with all of us at this stage (though 'pashing on' was as close as any of us had been to the real thing, I'm sure!) We had a fascination with 'willies', mainly other people's ('willies' was the common name in Glasgow for men's sexual organs); one fellow in our class (who shall remain nameless) had a huge 'willie', or at least compared to the rest of us, and he would often be cajoled into showing it off in class…nothing queer about us!

The other place to 'inspect' 'willies' was the boy's urinal; there was always a rush to the 'lavy' when a boy with a (reputed) big 'willie' was spied going to the toilets! It was considered great fun when a crowd was in the toilets to rush in behind them and push them against the urinal while they were 'peeing'! The unlucky ones would emerge from the toilets with their pants wet and the playground would erupt in laughter (girls included!) It was always funny till it happened to you…and it usually did!

The playground toilets were also where we tried to spy on the girls (and vice versa) as the boys and girls toilets were only separated by one wall and there was always some part which was in need of repair…and thus good for spying!

Sometimes our group would amuse ourselves during the morning or afternoon break by singing the latest rock 'n' roll songs. We'd walk around the playground trying to harmonise like the 'Kingston Trio' did with their song, *Tom Dooley* or like the 'Everly Brothers'. One of our gang, Robert (Noble) was a fanatical 'Buddy Holly' fan, and when 'Buddy' died in the plane crash in '59, Robert convinced all of us to wear black ties to school as a sign of mourning.

Unfortunately for us it was Mr Sieth's turn on playground duty that day and he bailed us up and asked what the black ties were for. Robert piped up, "Buddy Holly died, Sir"…We never found out if Mr Sieth was a fan of 'Buddy Holly' or not, but we all got the belt and were sent home at lunchtime to change our ties!

This Robert was a bit of a lad and he and his pal (another Robert) were right into smoking (usually in the toilets during period breaks or on the way to and from school). They encouraged all our gang to try smoking, which most of us did, me included. My undoing was when Robert 'graduated' to smoking cigars. Walking home from school on one occasion he offered me a 'drag'; a little unsure I took a 'puff' held the smoke in my mouth then blew it out.

Rob wasn't impressed, "Do the drawback, like this!" he said and inhaled a mouthful of the cigar smoke, blowing it out with a nonchalant air after a few moments…Well, I tried to follow his example. I inhaled the smoke and nearly choked to death, turning green at the same time! I suppose, in one way, I had Robert to thank that I never seriously took up smoking (cigarettes or cigars) after that incident.

I didn't give up my connection with the weed entirely though, as I sometimes bought and sold cigarettes. I was always on the lookout to make more 'pocket money' as mine never seemed to be enough, and at that time you could buy a packet of five 'Wills Woodbine' for a shilling. I'd buy a packet, when I could afford it, then sell the cigarettes individually for threepence each, making a profit of threepence on each pack. There were always boys at school who, while they couldn't afford to buy a pack of cigarettes, could always find the money for one. Smoking was one of the 'social graces' in those days, unlike now.

Speaking of being always on the lookout for more pocket money, my friend Hamish, who always seemed to have money to burn, would often ask me to double him home on my bike after school for which he would sometimes give me a couple of bob (two shillings). On other occasions, he would 'bribe' me with a plastic motor vehicle (somewhat like Dinky Toys) which were very popular at the time. All this helped keep me solvent in times of need!

The unfortunate side was that my bike ended up the worst of wear from this continual doubling of my pal and I was for ever fixing punctures or bent spokes. The matter was resolved, however, when Dad bought me a 'policeman's bike'! This was an old-fashioned metal framed bike built like a tank, which was too large for me as I could hardly reach the pedals from the seat.

Painted black, the bike looked just like the one used by the police to patrol the neighbourhood, hence the tag, 'policeman's bike'. With most of the other boys who rode to school doing so on racing bikes like 'Raleigh' or 'Flying Scots', I came in for a fair share of good humoured banter from my pals, which was in part instrumental to my walking to and from school. Dad couldn't understand why I was reluctant to use the bike and my pal Hamish had to use 'Shank's pony' (walk) to get home from school.

While I was never a model pupil at school and got into my share of trouble, I never missed much schooling in my four years at Victoria Drive, maybe it had something to do with my grandfather (Papa Winton) being a truant officer!

Scouting for Boys and Girls!

It was said that in the '50s, the Scottish education system was the best in the world….pity that I didn't take more advantage of it! However, it was through scouting that I gained most of my skills and confidence that stood by me throughout the rest of my life.

My pals, Brian (Cheyne) and Barry (Patrick), introduced me to scouting by taking me to join the 110th Scouts Cub Pack not long after my family moved to Dykebar Avenue.

I was soon into the rough and tumble of cubs, enjoying the games and companionship as well as learning skills and gaining badges in a variety of disciplines. I still managed to get into trouble, though and was severely reprimanded by Akela for starting a scuffle with another cub, not long after I joined! But the discipline was good for me and in time I became a 'sixer' (leader of a group of six cubs) before graduating to the scouts a few years later.

The 110th Boy Scout Troop had its' own scout hall in some vacant land not far from where I lived. The area was shared with vegetable and flower gardens and was bounded by the railway line on one side and major roads on two others. The advantage of this was we could make as much noise as we wanted without creating problems for neighbours.

The troop met on Friday nights and was made up of around sixty boys between the ages of twelve and eighteen years. The boys came from around the area or went to the same schools, so we were a close-knit group. We also had good leaders who were keen on the development of the boys under their charge.

The troop had great rivalry with the local boys brigade company of the area, and while we could match them in most things, they were far superior in marching which always gave us a showing up when both groups were involved in a parade or church service. My pal Barry and I decided to rectify this on the occasion we were designated to carry the 'colours' (flags) at a church service.

We had our patrol practice marching for weeks leading up to the service, and on the day we thought we performed the slow march quite well; this was confirmed when congratulations were passed on to us by the Minister…we were well pleased feeling that was 'one in the eye' for the boys brigade.

Our scout nights, when not given over to special activities (like learning to march) could become quite boisterous at times with games such as 'British bulldog', 'countries' or 'brandings' being played with vigour. The floor of our scout hall was of concrete and coming in contact with it could leave you with a bruise or two, especially when we played the game where we had scouts 'piggy-backing' another scout then fighting to 'unhorse' their opponent. I'd often return home after a thoroughly enjoyable night with the skin off my knees and elbows and my uniform in need of repair…or at the very least a good wash (luckily, scouting taught you how to wash and mend your own clothes!).

One of my pals, Brian (Morton) collided with another scout while playing 'British bulldog' and ended up with a broken hand! Brian was one of the feisty characters of the troop who never gave an inch when involved in competition, so some of us were quite pleased with his misfortune, which kept his hand in plaster and him on the side line for a few weeks!

Of course, we also had quieter periods during our troop night when we'd study for badges or have games of skill involving; observation, knot tying, first aid bandaging or cooking and camping skills, to name but a few. These skills stood me in good stead when Dad took us on climbing weekends.

We also spent time organising for our yearly 'gang show' which was always popular with our families and friends. Nearly all of the scouts, as well as some of the Cubs and Rovers scouts, had a part to play in these shows, whether in front of the stage or behind it.

Our hall was always packed when we put on a show, and while one of our groups would be entertaining the audience the rest of us would be out the back in a temporary hut putting on greasepaint and costumes and having a last minute look at our lines. The huts were heated with a pot-bellied stove and the mixture of smoke, greasepaint and a crowd of scouts in different stages of undress, laughing and joking made for great companionship.

At the end of the evening the whole troop would be on stage singing the scouts anthem of "We're riding along on the crest of a wave" to thunderous applause. After the curtain calls, we'd all be back out in the cosy warmth of the hut sipping hot 'namco' (scouts name for hot chocolate – national milk and cocoa) and reliving the highlights of the night.

Our gang show was only a small version of the Glasgow Gang Show which was performed in the city each year by scouts selected from all the troops in Glasgow. It was a big event and drew an audience from all over Scotland and was something to which the more dramatically minded in the troop aspired.

My time with the scouts also raised my awareness of the 'opposite sex'; this was no doubt helped by the fact that we had a 'sister' troop of girls guides with whom we held dances and parties during the year. Our Christmas party was the one we most looked forward to, as not only did we have dances but we also played a number of party games of which 'postman's knock' was by far the favourite! This 'game' gave both boys and girls the opportunity to get a kiss from their 'heartthrob'…provided they picked the right number! And as the kiss was behind closed doors, it could sometimes go on for ever…however, if the wrong number was chosen there would be squeals of dismay and the 'postman' would get short shrift!

But overall, the nights were great fun and there was always competition at the end of the evening as the scouts vied to take their favourite girl home.

The troop also held dances which were open to all the youngsters of the area and there was always great demand for tickets, as these were limited. Of course, the scouts got the first option on tickets which made us very popular with the girls! On the nights of the dances, the scout hall would be packed with up to a hundred and fifty youngsters dancing to the latest 'pop' music or skiffle group.

'Skiffle' was very big in Glasgow in this period with Lonnie Donegan's *'Rock Island Line'* and *'Cumberland Gap'* topping the charts. Our Rover Scouts had their own skiffle group led by Ronnie Morton which was always well received at these dances.

There was seldom any trouble at the dances as they were well supervised by the scoutmasters and rover scouts, the trouble usually arose over who was taking who home. On one such occasion, one of our troop was badly beaten up on his way home as he'd taken another fellow's girl (the fellow was not a scout). After this incident, consideration was given to stopping the dances. But happily, this did not happen and there were no further incidents of this type.

The funds raised through the dances were used for a variety of purposes, among other things we'd make up Christmas hampers which were distributed to the needy of the area through our local minister. The troop also raised funds for this cause through whist drives, garden fetes, jumble sales etc., all this was in addition to the regular 'bob-a-job' fundraising.

Camping was a regular activity of the troop and the Glasgow scouts were lucky to have a large campsite called Auchengillan, which we often went to as it was just near Loch Lomond. Auchengillen was used mainly for day camps or overnight bivouacs where the younger scouts coming through the organisation could learn the basic skills of camping and cooking etc.

We would sometimes go there for 'wide games' which were played at night and were somewhat like a version of 'hide-and-seek' (more like search and destroy!) where patrols were set against each other. We would return from such evenings tired and exhausted, covered in dirt or mud and with a few scrapes and bruises but having had a great time.

On one occasion, my pal Brian and I jumped the boundary fence (despite the warning that at no time were the boundaries of the camp to be crossed) and spent the afternoon in the adjacent field taking 'pot shots' at rabbits with a slug gun. (Auchengillan was alive with rabbits).

Unfortunately for us, Brian's brother, Ronnie, who was our assistant scout master caught us (most likely because he'd done the same thing himself!) and confined us to camp and we had to do the washing up and latrine duties…so much for the rabbit stew we thought we'd be having! (What's the point of having a big brother if he's a scoutmaster!)

My first 'real' scout camp was quite an experience for me, as a new camper I, along with the other first-time campers, was given all the worst jobs to do as well as being put through the initiation ceremonies. The worst chore was the digging of the camp latrines and then being responsible for looking after them, ugh!

We also had to fetch the water for the camp each day as well as gather the firewood (it was all open cooking, not a primus stove in sight!) We would be woken up at an ungodly hour by one of the rover scouts and be off into the woods while the frost was still on the ground and the mist in the air (if it wasn't raining!) to fetch the firewood and water before the rest of the camp was awake.

One morning it was colder and more miserable than usual. One of our group refused to get out of his sleeping bag; next minute two of the rover scouts 'emptied' him out of his bag and frog marched him over to the showers area and dowsed him with freezing cold water! Worst was to come; later on that day, they staked this unfortunate character out on the ground with nothing on (luckily, it had warmed up and the sun was out) and smeared his private parts with jam, and told him that the forest ants would smell the jam and come and 'nibble' at him! Of course, they were only joking and they released him after a couple of hours, but it did impress on this luckless scout who should be obeyed and he didn't neglect his duties for the rest of that camp!

As usual, I didn't learn from his mistake and it wasn't long before I was in trouble for refusing an order from these same rover scouts! They grabbed me early one morning, and marched me (naked) to an old horse trough which was full of green slimy water…and freezing cold! Standing me at one end of the trough they took my arms and attempted to make me walk the length of the trough which was about eight feet long and eighteen inches deep. I of course resisted, but as they exerted pressure on my arms I was forced into the trough, lost my footing on the slimy bottom and ended up getting a ducking! I didn't know whether to laugh or cry as I stood there dripping in slime and shivering…

Fortunately, the rovers knew I'd had enough and they wrapped me in a camp blanket and hurried me over to the blazing campfire. While I got cleaned up and warm in front of the fire, they brought my clothes to me…they felt I had learned my lesson, and I had!

Despite these incidents, we always had a great time at camps and the campfires at night were always the highlight where we sat and watched the sparks fly up and disappear into a night sky filled with stars while singing our scouting songs with a mug of hot namco in our hands.

In '57, the World Scout Jamboree was to be held at Sutton Coalfields in England (just outside Manchester) and our troop, along with all the other troops in Glasgow, was invited to nominate scouts to attend as part of the Glasgow contingent. The prerequisite was that all scouts had to have their Queen Scout badge and be aged fifteen years or over.

The Jamboree was to celebrate the centenary of Baden Powell's birth and fifty years of scouting – The Jubilee Jamboree!

Of course, I was keen to go despite not yet being fifteen and still to attain my Queen Scout badge; our skipper felt that I could qualify with a bit of luck. So, I was nominated along with my pal Barry and Ronnie Morton (who at this stage had not yet become an assistant scout master) and his pal, Drew Nichol.

We were all accepted for the Glasgow contingent and I had to knuckle down and undertake the tasks and tests to gain my Queen Scout badge before the Jamboree in August, which I did becoming one of the youngest Queen Scouts and one of the youngest scouts at the Jamboree – though I was to learn later that there was an eleven year old Dutch scout at the event because he played in a band!

The skipper was a little disappointed that I didn't take part in the formal ceremony to be presented with my Queen Scout badge, preferring to have it conferred on me at our own troop night. This may also have had something to do with me having a date on the formal presentation night…at fourteen, plus my priorities were already with the opposite sex!!!

Once accepted for the Jamboree, our group became part of the Glasgow contingent and we were required to attend meetings on a regular basis leading up to the event. These meetings always commenced with an inspection of our uniforms, which had to be of the highest standard.

At one of the early meetings, Barry was bawled out because he had turned the bottom of his shorts up a couple of times to take them off his knees. This was something we had being doing for some time at our troop, because, I think, we thought it looked smart and our shorts didn't flap around our knees – the bawling out put an end to that!

We had to be kitted out in the contingent's uniform (which we had to buy) and we all had to wear kilts. I was lucky in as much as I had my father's kilt from the Gordon Highlanders, which with a bit of adjustment fitted me fine. The contingent's tartan was the MacLean which we wore as our neckties.

Most of the meetings were taken up with protocol and information about the Jamboree as well as marching (those in charge were obviously aware of our shortfalls in this area!). By July, we were a well drilled group and ready for the big event.

The World Scout Jamboree was opened on 1st of August by the Duke of Gloucester with over thirty-five thousand scouts in attendance from eighty-two countries around the world…it was bigger than Ben Hur!

Our Glasgow contingent had its camp next to the South African and American contingents and we quickly made friends in both camps, though we were to 'take the mickey' out of the Americans on numerous occasions they being so gullible.

I became quite friendly with a number of the South African scouts, one in particular, Peter Burnette from King Williams Town, Cape Province, gave me his South African contingent songbook as a souvenir which I still have to this day (this was only issued to the South African Scouts attending the Jamboree).

For a number of years following the Jamboree, I corresponded with some of the South African boys.

'Swapping' was one of the events at the Jamboree that almost every scout got involved with, and the Glasgow contingent was no exception. Anything and everything was there to be swapped, especially in the eyes of the American scouts! Though, all scouts were directed not to swap any part of their uniform, many did…our kilts were all the rage and some of our lads got as much as thirty pounds for their kilt, which was a lot of money in those days. While I had offers to sell mine and was sorely tempted I felt I couldn't as it belonged to my father.

The American scouts were unbelievable in their quest for souvenirs which led to a very funny incident with some of them when we were erecting our entrance into our campsite. We had just finished erecting the poles at the entranceway and had stretched some tartan cloth between them and were in the process of lacquering the material to make it weatherproof when a group of American scouts came by.

Seeing what appeared to be two of our scouts applying tartan paint to a piece of material, they at once wanted to know where they could get some. Unfortunately, for the 'yanks' the two scouts were Ronnie Morton and Drew Nichol, who were always on the lookout for some fun!

At first, we thought they were joking, then realising they were serious it was explained to them that you could only get tartan paint in Scotland and it could never be taken out of the country, but we had received special permission because of the Jamboree. Ronnie also told them that we were not allowed to sell any of it or give it away as it was a secret process perfected in Scotland and it all had to be accounted for when we got back to Scotland.

Well, by this time the 'yanks' were hooked and were desperate to get a tin of tartan paint. Eventually, Ronnie and Drew let them wear them down and they sold them the remains of a tin on the proviso that they hid it while in camp and didn't open it till after they got back home from the Jamboree. I often wonder what our fellow American scouts thought of us when they got 'back home'! (And I never found out what Ronnie and Drew did with their 'ill gotten' gains!)

Our American friends were by far the most gullible of the scouts at the Jamboree and we just couldn't help but have them on (it might have been something to do with them sleeping on camp beds and mattresses while we roughed it on the ground!) We would regale them with stories about the highlands of Scotland and the weird and wonderful things to be found there such as the 'haggis' bird that lived on the mountaintops and was a ferocious predator.

With the Americans being taken in by the 'haggis' tales we decided to create a 'haggis' bird. We built a cage and covered the bottom of it with earth and straw, then placed a sporran filled with dirt and with feathers sticking out of it at the back of the cage, mostly hidden behind the earth and straw. The cage was placed in a dimly lit part of one of our tents and we put a sign outside inviting scouts to come in and view the 'haggis' bird!

While most scouts saw this as a joke and went along with it, some of our American friends were convinced that there was 'something' in the cage. We would never let any of the scouts get too close to the cage as we had the area roped off and we 'stood guard'!

As each day passed the stories of the 'Haggis' bird got more and more fanciful till it got to the stage where we felt we couldn't keep the pretence up anymore without being found out…so we decided to let the 'haggis' escape!

Next morning before reveille, we went running through the campsite yelling, "The haggis bird has escaped! The haggis bird has escaped!" Well, you had to be there to see the effect on the American scouts. They took off in all directions with the fear of death in their faces while we all collapsed in a heap with laughter! Lucky for us the American scouts were good at sports and once realising they had been got at they saw the funny side too – which in a way was lucky for us, as we could have got ourselves into serious trouble for pulling such a prank!

However, there was one area that the American scouts left all others for dead in and that was in 'swapping'. We were often overawed and amazed at the organised way the Americans went about swapping; some of them had bags full of badges, pins and assorted items for swapping, and they would stop at nothing when they saw an item they wanted…I know because it happened to me!

I had just swapped one of my tartan neckties with a Canadian scout for a beautifully carved woggle of a moose head resplendent with antlers. When I was approached by an American scout who asked me what I wanted for the woggle, I said it wasn't for swapping as I had just swapped my necktie for it and wanted to keep it. But the American persisted, he told me that his nickname was 'Moose' (what else, being a yank!) and he just had to have the woggle. He laid out all his swaps and said I could have my pick of any or all of them as long as he got the woggle.

Well, either he was a very good salesman or I was wet behind the ears (the latter I think!) for at the end, I relented and swapped my moose head for his United States Scout Jamboree necktie and woggle (which I still have today).

The Jamboree had many important people visit including the Queen and the Duke of Edinburgh as well as the Prime Minister of Britain. It was a great thrill for the scouts as these dignitaries mingled with them and spoke to the lucky few. Lord Rowallan, the chief scout of the United Kingdom, was present at the Jamboree, and it was decided to give him a gift from all the scouts of the United Kingdom, Commonwealth and Empire contingents; for this, each scout of the contingent had to donate a penny.

Our gift was a portrait of Lord Rowallan in his chief scout uniform – I thought this was rather a poor choice at the time, but for a penny I wasn't game to comment!

Each day of the Jamboree was highly organised from 'camp rise' at 7 am to 'flag fall' at 10 pm, though we had plenty of free time to do our own thing (like making haggis birds!) provided we passed the morning inspection of our camp. My aunt May (mum's sister) lived in Manchester and visited the Jamboree to see me. I got permission to leave the camp on that day and had a lovely time with my aunt and a slap up meal into the bargain! No camp food for me that day! (not that the camp food wasn't up to standard, most days it was excellent!)

The first week of the Jamboree the weather was fine, in fact, we had a heatwave for a couple of days and there was some concern that the perishable foodstuff might go bad (there was no refrigeration on site). Luckily, this didn't eventuate as on the second week it poured! Typical British weather! It rained so bad that some campsites were washed away along with some of the American scouts on their inflatable mattresses! In our camp, we were up to our ankles in mud, it was rather a sad ending to wonderful two weeks!

On 13th of August, the last of the scout contingents left camp to return to their homeland with memories that would last them a lifetime.

In '59, our troop, the 110th Glasgow, celebrated twenty-one years of scouting and a special dinner was held at a function centre opposite the Odeon Picture House at Anniesland Cross. The picture showing was titled *'A Night To Remember'* (about the sinking of the Titanic) which was very appropriate to our celebration.

This year also saw our troop start its own newsletter which was called *'The 110th Rag'*, no doubt a play on a popular jazz tune of that era. Fifty copies of the 'rag' were printed and all sold at tuppence each! As one of the senior scouts and a patrol leader by this time, I was assigned the role of a reporter for our cub pack which gave me my first taste of 'copywriting' and the opportunity to see my name in print, though the quality of my first article may have left much to be desired! In the March issue of the 'rag', I penned my first story (outside of the cub activities).

This came about when only six cubs turned up for their activities, due to the cold, snowy and bleak February evening. Because it was so cold, Akela sent the cubs home early and the group leaders and I adjourned to the scout hall's kitchen for a 'cuppa'. Unfortunately, when we turned the taps on there was no water, the cold outside had frozen the water pipes!

Remembering the scout's motto, "Be Prepared", one of the assistant cub masters grabbed a dixie from the cupboard and went outside and filled it with snow. Returning triumphantly he said, "Light the stove, we'll soon have hot water for our tea in no time!" We all waited expectantly as the kettle began to boil…unfortunately once boiled all that came out of it was about half an inch of dirty grey water! Needless to say, we all went home without our 'cuppa'…but I had got my first scoop for *The 110th Rag*!

In April'59, I had to say 'goodbye' to the 110th as my family left Scotland for Australia, but the lessons I learnt from my days in the scouts stood me well for the future and the 110th Glasgow Boy Scout Troop will always remain a fond memory to me.

Holidays Were Happy Days!

As far back as I can remember our family always went on family holidays which was not the case with many families of Glasgow. We were one of the lucky ones and no matter where we went or with whom, we always had a great time…as is borne out with these snippets from the past.

Dad's love of the Highlands was matched only by his love for travel, and the early years of my childhood were spent with my family (and sometimes relatives) in the Highlands of Scotland…prior to this, in my very early years, I spent my holidays at Rothesay where my Granma and Papa Winton rented a holiday flat.

While I can remember little of these years, I can recall Rothesay Castle quite clearly as it stood across the road from where we stayed. The castle was an impressive sight even though some of its walls were crumbling, it had a moat around its perimeter which abounded in wildfowl. On wet and windy days, I would often gaze out of the window at Rothesay Castle, dreaming of bygone battles, while Granma Winton would make the best pancakes on her big iron griddle which hung permanently above the open fireplace.

The fireplace was built in the old style and you could sit inside it with the fire blazing merrily in the centre which was just wonderful on cold days. I'd often sit in the heat of the hearth eating Granma's hot pancakes with lashings of real butter and homemade jam while supping on a hot cup of cocoa.

When I was just a 'toddler', Papa would often take me walking along the promenade at Rothesay, which was a popular pastime for all the holidaymakers, though the outfits were much different from today. Men would be dressed in their three-piece suits with waistcoats and hats while the ladies would be dressed to the 'nines'.

As I got older, Mum would take me to pick brambles in the Skipper Woods in the hills behind the town. I'd eat as many as I picked and would often end up with a pain in the 'peeny' (tummy)! Both Mum and Granma would make homemade bramble jam from these outings which was just magic on a jeely piece.

My first holiday which I can vaguely recall with Mum and Dad was at Portgordon in '48. We stayed in a small cottage in the village right on the quayside. I recall that my bed was built into a cavity of the wall and I could look out the small window and watch the fishing fleet come and go while other fishermen would be sitting on the quayside mending their nets or sorting fish into wooden boxes filled with ice, ready for the markets.

Port Gordon is a small fishing village near the entrance to the Moray Firth, situated on Spey Bay about twenty miles west of Banff. This was my first experience of this part of Scotland and I was enthralled with the quaint seaside village and the wide countryside beyond, much different from 'dirty old Glesga'.

In '49, Dad, as part of his training in youth work had to attend a camp in the Lake District of England and he took the family with him. Dad rented a caravan for Mum, me and Alastair (who was only a baby), in a field close by the manor house where his training was taking place. We hadn't settled into the caravan very long when I caused havoc by knocking the tops off the ant's nests in the field around our caravan and we were invaded by flying ants! These ants were everywhere and got into everything! Mum was nearly demented as the ants even got into the baby's cot and were all over Alastair…Luckily, no harm was done, but I was told not to interfere with such things in the future!

The Lake District was also where I learned to swim, albeit by accident! There was a man-made rock pool at the bottom of the meadow where we were staying and I used to go there regularly. The water, though quite deep, was crystal clear and I would sit and watch the small fish and water insects darting about. One day, I got too engrossed in my watching and overbalanced and fell into the pond! As there was no one around to save me, I somehow managed to 'dog-paddle' to the edge of the pool and scramble out – Mum was amazed when I came home to the caravan wet through and announced I could now swim!

While Mum, Alastair and I were amusing ourselves in the countryside around the lake, Dad would be off on climbing expeditions with the youth group for which he was responsible; this was all part of his training. Towards the end of our stay, Dad took the group sailing on Lake Windermere and we went along. It was my first time on a sail boat and I was fascinated by the wind in the sails and the sound of the water as it lapped along the side of the yacht, it was a pleasant ending to an enjoyable holiday.

The following year saw us at Port Appin, where we rented what was called in Scotland a wee 'but and ben' – a small cottage. The cottage was situated on the edge of Loch Linnhe, a beautiful area on the west coast of the highlands. By day I'd watch the seals playing in the waters off the Lynne of Lorne, while by night there would be magnificent skies as the sun set behind the Western Isles.

One day while out walking with Dad, I came across an Adder (Scotland's only poisonous snake) which was sunning itself in the grass. Having never seen a snake before, I went to pick it up and was only saved from a nasty accident when Dad, seeing what I was about to do, flicked the snake away with his walking staff!

The small village of Port Appin had only one general store, which fascinated me as it sold everything imaginable from haberdashery to fruit and vegetables as well as having a section for ice cream and sweeties. I spent many hours in this little store taken in by its smells and of course spending every penny I had on sweeties or chewing gum.

Chewing gum was quite a novelty in the early '50s (bubble gum had not yet come onto the market) and I'd buy packet after packet of it, much to Mum's distaste! There was a popular tune at that time called *"Chew, chew, chew, chew chewing gum, how I love chewing gum"* which I'm sure had a lot to do with my fascination of this product.

Granma and Granpa Waddell came and stayed with us at Port Appin, which is the only time I remember Granpa Waddell being away from his hearth at Carntyne, though he still managed to read the papers and fall asleep in front of the fire!

In '51, we holidayed at Arbroath on Scotland's East coast, just up from Dundee, where Dad's brother, Uncle Bruce, his wife, Aunt Margaret, and my cousin, Elizabeth, joined us. Elizabeth and I were much the same age (I being only a couple of weeks older than her) and we spent many hours playing on the sands and searching for crabs under the clumps of seaweed when the tide went out. More than once I got my fingers nipped by crabs when I was too eager in my exploring under the seaweed!

One evening during our stay there, was a tremendous storm with torrential rain and forked lighting flashing across the skies. We were watching the effects of the storm on the seas from our living room window when we saw a distress flare light up the sky. We could just make out a boat out at sea floundering in the huge waves. Next to our place was the boatshed which held the lifeboat, and as we watched the seamen in their bright yellow souwesters jumped into the boat as it went down its slipway and hit the sea throwing up spray everywhere.

We watched as the lifeboat disappeared into the storm heading for the vessel in distress. It was too dark for us to see the outcome of the attempted rescue, but we learned next day that the lifeboat had managed to rescue the crew off the ship but the ship had foundered. This bit of excitement gave me much to talk about at school when we returned from our holiday.

We returned to the East coast the following year to stay at Carnoustie, a small fishing village on the Tayside. Alastair and I tried our hand at the putting greens at the village. We were unaware at the time of Carnoustie being famous for its golf course; not that it would have made much difference to us. I mainly remember this holiday for the weather which was windy and cold and we were in raincoats most of the time.

In '53, we holidayed at Anstruther, again on the East coast of Scotland not far from St. Andrews. On the way, we visited some of Dad's relatives who lived at Lundin Links. We spent a pleasant afternoon playing croquet on their lawn while Lana and Fiona (who were only toddling at this stage) chased our host's bantam chickens all over the yard!

While at Anstruther we spent a day at Pittenweem, another quaint fishing village just south of where we were staying. Both Anstruther and Pittenweem date back from the medieval days and were well known for their catches of herring. We dined on this fine fish on many occasions.

'Smokies' were the famous fish of this area, so-called because the herring were salted and hung from the wooden beams of the small low roofed fish shops where they were then 'smoked' from the fumes of wood fires and sawdust. Smokies just melted in your mouth; they were a far different taste from Glasgow's famous 'fish suppers'.

Anstruther was to be the last of our Scottish holidays as the following year we started going to Europe, with Denmark our first overseas experience. (This followed the Danish Girls Choirs visit to us in '53.)

Denmark was a great new adventure! It was the first time us kids had been to a foreign country with people speaking a language we couldn't understand – thankfully quite a few of our Danish friends spoke English!

Dad had organised the trip to Denmark with a group of people from the community centre; some of who had hosted the Danish girls and their entourage the year before. As an 'exchange' visit, our group would be billeted with families in and around Copenhagen.

Our adventure started when we boarded the North Sea ferry at Southampton for our overnight voyage to Denmark. Once into the North Sea, the weather turned for the worst and in no time our ferry was battling stormy seas with high winds and rain squalls.

On the first night when we went to dinner, the movement of the ship made it almost impossible to eat the food as the plates kept sliding off the table! Next morning at breakfast, only a hardy few turned up! Most were in bed being sea sick (me included!). The weather got so bad and the seas so rough that all passengers were confined below decks for the remainder of the trip; it was a relief when we tied up safely at Copenhagen Harbour!

Our party was met by our Danish friends and soon we were all off to our respective 'homes' for the next few days. Our family went to stay with the Johanssons (who had stayed with us the previous year) who had a lovely home at Hvidore just outside of Copenhagen.

It was at the Johanssons that I first experienced a 'smorgasbord'; breakfast was a table laden with fruit, cheeses and pastries, hot rolls and coffee...beats porridge any day!

The Johanssons had three children, two boys and a girl, and I would go with the boys (Torgan and Kirk) to the local park and play football with them and their friends. It was quite an experience not understanding the language and having the boys yelling instructions to me and me yelling back! Just as well they played 'fitba' with the same rules as we did!

Our hosts had arranged a number of excursions for our group and on these days the groups would all meet up and be taken by coach around Copenhagen.

On of our first visits was to the Tivoli Gardens which really enthralled us as we had nothing like them in Scotland. In some way, they were like the forerunner to the theme parks of Disneyland and the like. We also visited the zoo, which was quite different to ours, and Lana and Fiona had their first rides on elephants.

A day at a cultural centre where we watched national dances was followed by a visit to the world famous 'The Little Mermaid' in Copenhagen Harbour where we had our photograph taken, with Alastair and me in kilts, as usual!

Denmark and the city of Copenhagen seemed so clean compared to Glasgow...but the weather was much the same! Thank goodness our trip home across the North Sea was all 'smooth sailing'!

What a different holiday in '55! Sunny Italy and ten days in Rome! (and at least with the hot weather Alastair and I got out of wearing our kilts!) This wasn't an 'exchange' holiday as at this stage Dad had not made any contacts in Italy. So our 'home' was in a large convent in the centre of Rome which the nuns of the convent ran as a hostel for tourists.

While I had some pals in Glasgow who were Catholics, Scotland was mainly a protestant country and Catholics were a minority, thus I had never pondered much on their religion. Rome was an eyeopener for me; there were 'religious' people everywhere! Nuns, Priests, Abbots, Brothers, Friars, all in their respective habits, and using every form of transport and with the general populous paying them as little attention as the next fellow.

As soon as you stepped outside of the peace and serenity of the convent, you were regaled with the noise and colour of the city – there appeared to be no traffic rules as small cars and motor scooters vied with the larger forms of transport for their right to the road, all with their horns blasting incessantly!

The females of our group soon became aware of the 'men' of Rome as they were continually having their bottoms 'pinched' as they walked down the streets!

At the convent, the nuns looked after our housekeeping and prepared and served our meals and, though they spoke little English and we almost no Italian, there were few communication problems. And perhaps it was as well they didn't understand too much of what we were saying as one of the lads in our group kept telling one of the pretty young novice nuns that he was going to pack her in his suitcase and take her home with him when we left!

This always brought a goodhearted laugh from our group as well as smiles from those nuns present; however it was the nuns who had the last laugh, though I'm sure they didn't realise it…it happened this way…

Our meals at the convent were always taken in a large dining room with long wooden tables in the centre and wooden benches on either side for us to sit on. This allowed our group to enjoy their repast together, usually with much frivolity and good humour.

At our first evening meal, the nuns place decanters of wine on the table and our lads, being Glaswegians, got 'stuck right into it', laughing and joking that it tasted like 'lolly water'. However it was much more potent than that as one by one our lads keeled over, much to the concern of our hostesses! There was much more care taken with the 'vino' after this episode!

One breakfast at the convent remains vividly in my mind, however, as instead of the usual fresh fruit, hot rolls and coffee, the nuns served us up what they told us was an Italian delicacy. To this day, I am unaware of what this delicacy was but it was brought out in large frying pans sizzling in oil and looked like some kind of vegetable such as cucumber or zucchini.

Most of our group took one, look at this and said, "No thanks!" but of course when it came to our end of the table and I refused, Dad told the nun to put it on my plate and said for me to eat it! (me and my vegetables, was I ever going to be free of them?)

Dad (and Alastair) having a cast iron stomach could eat anything, but this greasy, oily matter bubbling away in hot fat made my stomach turn! It was an unpleasant start to the day for me!

Our group did all the usual tourist things in Rome, visited the Trevi fountain and threw some coins in (weird for a Scotsman!), visited the Coliseum and the catacombs, the latter being quite amazing as the bones and skulls of the early Christians were still in their crypts.

We visited St. Peters Square which was packed with thousands of Christians, and we saw the reason when the Pope made an appearance high up in a window in the Vatican.

In the ruins of the Roman temples, I was amazed at the number and size of lizards which were everywhere. Alastair and I tried in vain to catch these, much to the amusement of our Italian guide. Ants too were everywhere, which was something else we were unaccustomed to in Scotland (cold weather may have some advantages!).

We spent a very pleasant day in the hills just behind Rome visiting the fountains of Rome. This was a beautiful area with fountains and waterfalls in all shapes and sizes. Our guide had great fun turning on fountains from hidden taps which would spray across the paths we were walking along; no one minded getting wet as in the hot Italian weather we not only got cooled down but our clothes dried almost instantaneously!

The weather in Rome was very hot and it took us some time getting used to it. Many of our group suffered from sunburn and heat exhaustion until we embraced the more leisurely pace of Italian life.

It was at the beach at Anzio that we were made very aware of the difference between a Scottish seaside resort and an Italian one…the sands were so hot we couldn't walk on them! The girls in our group thought this wonderful as they were carried across the sands to the warm Mediterranean Sea in the arms of the good looking Italian men…The males in our group were not so enamoured though, as they too had to be carried!

Anzio was the first place that I experienced surf and it was quite scary at first as the waves were quite strong and pummelled us onto the shore, but the warmth of the water soon overcame our fears and in no time we were enjoying ourselves and frolicking in the waves.

Of course no trip to Rome would be complete without a visit to the Vatican, so like all good tourists we made our way to St. Peters. Once inside we gazed in awe at the magnificence of the building…though this didn't faze my little sister, Fiona, who broke away from Mum's hand and ran to kneel at the altar of St. Peter (Fiona was all of four years old at this stage!)

I also was overcome by my surroundings and decided to purchase a gift for Mum. I bought a lovely (to me) white beaded necklace with my pocket money and presented it to Mum, which she accepted graciously…it wasn't till years afterwards that she told me the 'necklace' I gave her was actually rosary beads! (and me a 'Proddy' too!)

We had a wonderful time in Italy and returned to Scotland vowing we'd go back again…it was to be thirty five years before I fulfilled that vow…

The following year saw us back again in Europe and I had my first flight in an aeroplane as we flew KLM Airways to Holland. What a difference to our North Sea crossing to Denmark! Though our plane did hit a few air pockets, the trip was short and uneventful and we landed at Schiphol Airport to be greeted by our Dutch hosts. Schiphol Airport was quite an amazing place as the four types of transport (road, rail, sea and sky) were all to be seen side by side, due in part to the extensive canal systems of Holland.

This was our second 'exchange' visit as the previous year we had hosted a group from Holland and they were now reciprocating.

On this occasion, I was to be billeted with Joosten family (it was their son Bob who came to stay with us in Glasgow in later years) while the rest of my family went to stay with the group leader of the Dutch contingent. As the Joostens lived a little way from where the rest of our party was billeted, I had quite a bit of time to myself, only meeting up with the rest of the group when we had organised excursions.

One such outing was to the model village of Madurodam. We spent a fascinating afternoon there walking around the model village with its scale models of Dutch buildings and model boats plying up and down the canals. We had nothing to compare with this in Scotland and it kept us enthralled for hours.

While Madurodam was one of my many memories of Holland along with the windmills and canals, my most vivid memory is of breakfasts at the Joostens, as instead of porridge I was given the choice of fresh-baked bread spread with what the Dutch called 'mouches' – chocolate sprinkles or coloured sprinkles...I thought all my Christmases had come at once!

I returned to Holland the next year, this time with the Knightswood Pipe Band, while the rest of the family went to Switzerland. The girls Scottish country dance group also came along with the band which was one of the reasons I was anxious to go with band (I wasn't a great piper).

Our group stayed at a hotel in The Hague and it was all our leaders could do to keep us from getting up to mischief; we were nearly thrown out of the hotel on a number of occasions due to our 'high jinks'. One such incident saw us 'partying' in the girls rooms (males and females were in separate areas of the hotel) when the hotel manager burst in on us and there were bodies going everywhere!

Some of us hid in cupboards (and were caught) while some lads took their chances and jumped off the balcony (luckily these were only a few feet off the ground!) We were all given a stern warning by our leaders, but that didn't stop us!

We would also go down to the beach at night and make use of the small portable 'change rooms' for 'winching'...and be chased back to the hotel by the watchman!

It was not all fun and frivolity as we were given a civic reception by the Burgermaster of The Hague and we marched to the sound of our pipes and drums in full regalia from the hotel to the reception at the town hall. While the Dutch had seen bagpipes before (as they themselves played what they called the 'doodlesak') they were obviously not used to kilts and as we marched along, the children would dart out from the crowds on the pavements and flick up our kilts then dart back again screaming with laughter! Our Country Dance girls were quite amused but not so some of us! But the reception was excellent and our piping much appreciated by the guests.

Another incident of a light hearted nature that befell us on this holiday happened when we went to a picture house to see *'Jailhouse Rock'*. There were signs on the walls of the theatre which said 'Verboden te Roken', which we thought meant that there was to be no rocking and rolling in the aisles during the show (this had been quite a common occurrence in theatres in Britain.) We found out differently, however, when a few of us went to light up our 'fags' and were ejected from the picture house! – the signs were 'No Smoking' signs!

That holiday in Holland was one never to be forgotten! It was on this trip that I became very fond of one of the girls (Irene) from the country dance team and most of the holiday I was vying for her attention along with one of the older lads from the band. While it was a bit 'touch and go' during the time in Holland as to who was winning her favours, when we returned to Scotland, Irene and I started 'going together' and became quite close.

I had quite mixed feelings when I had to say 'goodbye' to her some eighteen months later when my family and I sailed for Australia.

'58 was our last holiday before leaving for Australia; it was also the first holiday that Mum and Dad had without us kids. While we holidayed in Scotland with Granma and Grampa Waddell, they went to Spain.

In '59, Dad had arranged for a group to tour Iceland but our family didn't make it, instead we set out on our greatest holiday of all, six weeks aboard the TSS Strathaird as we sailed for our new home in Australia...

Porridge, Mince and Tatties, Cod Liver Oil and Sugarolly Water!

Growing up in Scotland after World War II, food shortages were still prevalent and the diet of the 'ordinary folk' consisted of basic staple foods and what could be procured with the food stamps.

Glaswegian fare was mainly stews, soups and mince and tatties with such vegetables that were available thrown in…leftovers, if there were any, were usually made into 'stovies' or 'toad-in-the-hole' for the next day.

Mind you, Glasgow 'fish and chips' were the best in the world and always a treat; wrapped up in last nights' *Evening Citizen* with plenty of salt and vinegar they were a staple of the Glaswegian's diet – none of these chips and curry sauce which you get today!

Dad, because of his experiences in the Low Countries directly after the war, was more aware than most of the food shortage that the people in Holland and Belgium suffered, and how children especially 'survived' on food scraps that the allied soldiers left behind. Because of this Dad was determined that none of his family would waste food, and as youngsters we had to eat everything that was put before us on a plate.

Dad was also not into the new-fangled food like corn flakes, and such things as cereals or packet soup along with tomato sauce and the likes were not to be found in our house. We started the day off with porridge – winter and summer…made with salt and definitely no sugar on it! I always felt it was unfair that my cousin Elizabeth (who was ages with me) was always allowed sugar with her porridge…

Nor were we allowed white bread, as Dad said it had too much sugar and starch in it and not enough grain (what must he think of today's 'white' bread when an experiment reported in the British medical journal stated that dogs fed exclusively on white bread died within two months of malnutrition!).

We were raised on brown wholemeal bread or, in our eyes what was worse, a Hovis loaf! This loaf you could bounce off the floorboards and it would be the floorboards which were dented! I'm sure it could have been used as bricks for building and no one would have been the wiser! I was pleased when I grew older and could make my own choice of brown bread!

In summertime, we would 'live' on Hovis bread sandwiches inches thick with home grown lettuce (Dad always had a garden full of lettuce, which by summers end we'd be thankful to see the last of! I'm sure rabbits ate less lettuce than what we did growing up!). Dad also grew tomatoes in the backyard and these supplemented the lettuce sandwiches on occasions along with cheese.

As well as such basic healthy food, we never went without our daily dose of cod liver oil in the winter months, ugh! The only thing that made this terrible tasting stuff palatable was the teaspoon of concentrated orange juice that (usually) went with it. Though, as much as I disliked those basic foodstuffs and the 'daily dose', I'm sure it was my growing up on such that helped give me the basis for my good health in later years.

As Dad would say, "You don't know what's good for you!" as I was always a little envious of my cousins and pals whose families were into the 'new-fangled food' as Dad called it.

I'd take every opportunity to visit my cousin Leslie who lived in Westerton (about three quarters of an hour bike ride away) to indulge in such 'forbidden fruits'! There, not only could I have a breakfast of cornflakes but also I could have tomato sauce on my scrambled egg! And if I stayed for tea I'd get chicken noodle soup – straight out of a packet! (this had only just come onto the market in the '50s).

It was the same at my cousin Elizabeth's home where, as I was given a choice of what I ate, every meal was a treat! I was always somewhat puzzled, however, that both my cousins, Elizabeth and Leslie, always loved to come to my place…I'm sure it wasn't for the food! As we grew up, a strong bond of friendship was forged between us which remains to this day.

While I did have my dislikes for Dad's policy on food, there were some meals that I did look forward to, mince and tatties being a favourite (provided I could 'dispose' of the vegetables!) I also liked black pudding and tripe, while peas brose was a nice change from porridge. Stovies too were popular if made with corned beef and potatoes, but add carrots or cabbage and leave me out! But my most favourite meal was the Thursday night's chips and eggs (deep fried); it was one meal I knew we wouldn't get vegetables with!

As I said in an earlier chapter, vegetables were my worst nightmare. Now and again when dad would catch me out trying to get rid of the veggies, he would watch over me until I had eaten the lot. This was worse than any punishment I could imagine.

Dad was also a 'teetotaller'. I don't think I ever saw him drink alcohol when we were growing up, not even at 'Ne'erday'. Dad told me in latter years that he had seen the effects of alcohol on his father and their family when he was growing up, and vowed he would not follow the same path.

For the festive season, Mum would make blackcurrant and ginger wine (non-alcoholic) which was a great favourite among all, even us kids. Mum would start making the wine around November, bottle it and give it time to settle before Christmas.

As I acquired a taste for the wine, I'd often sneak a few drinks prior to the bottle being opened then top the bottle up with water. As the basis of the wine was water and sugar with an essence added, provided I didn't overdo my indulgence, it usually went unnoticed. However, I think my brother and sisters were also onto this as they got older, and depending on which bottle of wine Mum opened first, she would sometimes exclaim, " Ooh, the wine is a bit weak this year…I must have added too much water" and knowing glances would be exchanged between us kids!

In the '50s, it was still quite common for women to make their own jams and condiments and Mum would make her share; our 'jeely pieces' (jam sandwiches) would have Mum's homemade jams on them for most of the year and though, we enjoyed these, we were sometimes pleased when plum jam came to an end!

In those days too, kids were also good at making their own soft drinks. Kids would make up real lemonade and sell the same to their less enterprising pals for two pence or three pence a glass on hot summer days, and if it had ice with it, heaven!

Sugarolly water was another favourite with youngsters, made from liquorice root it was somewhat similar to ginger beer without the fizzyness…it seems a pity that these skills have been lost to the present generation of youngsters…

Summertime, of course, was when the ice cream man came around and kids would swarm onto the streets when the Walls ice cream van or De Marcos would come into view playing *'Greensleeves'*. While a 'pokey hat' (ice cream cone) was always the favourite with the younger kids, wafers and 'double nougats' were all the go for the older kids or the ones with a few more pennies to spend.

The early '50s also saw the first milk based ice blocks come onto the market and these were an immediate success with the kids. Unfortunately, the manufacturers had not quite perfected the use of cold ice in the development of this treat and kids would get their tongue or lips 'stuck' to the ice block if they were not careful, which could be quite painful. Many a youngsters ended up with bleeding lips or mouth, in some cases kids were rushed to hospital to have the 'ice lolly' separated from their skin!...the popularity of this new treat, however, soon saw the problem overcome.

'Walls' ice cream was one of the first to sell their product through a cartoon strip in the daily newspaper, which they based on the concept of an adventure story centred around the 'lucky Walls' sign' (this sign was made by bringing your two thumbs together and having both forefingers pointing upward to form a *'W'*)

The children in the comic strip would get involved in some adventure, similar to the ones that faced Enid Blyton's *'Secret Seven'*, and when they got into a tight spot they'd invoke the lucky walls sign which would see them overcome the odds.

The 'lucky Walls' sign' became quite a cult for a few years and often us kids would bring the sign into our games that we played in the neighbourhood...

Our summers seemed much hotter and our winters colder, way back in the late '40s. The weather pattern has definitely shifted since I was a wee boy back then.

Often in summer, the days were so hot that the tar would melt on the footpaths and the roads, and us kids would have a great time gathering the tar and moulding it into toy soldiers, animals and the like, but woe betide you if you came home with tar on your clothing or shoes as it was impossible to get off without ruining the garment. I recall getting more than one 'skelping' for ruining my school shirt or pants with tar!

The other summer ritual was the visit to the barber shop, and I mention it here because of an incident that befell me on one such occasion.

Usually, me and my pals would go to the barber shop on a Saturday morning for our haircuts. You'd meet more pals on the way and by the time you got to the shop there would be kids everywhere. The barbers shop was a favourite meeting place where you could chat with your pals and catch up on the latest comics without the interference of adults! Barber's shops were always full on Saturdays and you could rely on being there up to a couple of hours before your turn came on the big chair.

The barber would place a wooden plank across the arms of the chair for you to sit on, so you were high enough up for him to work on your hair, and all the time he'd be doing it, your pals sitting waiting behind you would be making smart comments and when you tried to come back at them the barber would clip you on the ear (with his hand) to make you stay still…which would be the results your pals were looking for and they'd dissolve into laughter!

However, Dad was always unhappy about the times us kids 'wasted' at the barber shop, feeling we should be doing something more productive with our time. On one occasion, he gave me the money to go to the barbers on the way home from school. That afternoon, I was sauntering home from school making small talk with one of the girls from my class when I discovered a shilling in my pocket. I couldn't think where it came from, but with money in my hand and a girl at my shoulder, I thought here was an opportunity to make an impression.

Marzipan balls were a big treat with us kids in those days, so with a shilling in my pocket and walking right past the barber shop, I spent the lot on marzipan balls! I was a big hit with my lady friend! That night, when Dad got home from work he remarked, "That's not much of a haircut the barber gave you!" The penny dropped! Luckily, Dad must have been too preoccupied with other things as he didn't raise the matter again and I got off, as the saying goes 'scot-free'!

'Sweeties' were a weakness of mine as the above incident would attest and in Glasgow, we had great sweetie shops. I think it may have developed from the need to combat the dull grimness of the city and the long winters of those days… Black striped balls, aniseed balls, soor plooms, gobstoppers, toffees and chocolates, we had a lot and it was every kids treat on a Saturday to spend some of his or her money on a bag of sweeties.

We also had a taste for less common treats such as liquorice root, horlick tablets and cinnamon sticks – mind you, the day we tried smoking cinnamon sticks put us off them for a while!

By the late '50s, Dad had somewhat succumbed to the 'new-fangled food' and I could enjoy corn flakes and tomato sauce…but he still insisted we eat all our vegetables.

1957–59 Teenage Years and New Horizons

By the time I became a teenager, girls had become the major interest in my life, as was the same with most of my pals, some of whom had 'steady' girlfriends since high school, but not me; while I was more than interested in the 'opposite sex' I was still a bit unsure of myself in their company…this however, did not stop me from pursuing this 'interest'!

…And we had plenty of opportunity to mix with girls; local dances, scout and girl guide functions, parties and of course, before and after school there was always the opportunity to make up with the girls.

But the bane of our lives were the school dances. These were a bit of a *'Catch-22'* for us as while we enjoyed being with the girls, these dances and the preparation for them were a trial…

In the months leading up to the school dance, we'd find ourselves in the school gymnasium, boys on one side girls on the other and our music teacher in the middle (sometimes assisted by one of the male staff).

The teacher would usually start off by commenting on the 'scruffiness' of some of the boys which would bring giggles from the girls' side of the room…and would put us 'lads' at an immediate disadvantage. Comments like "Winton, don't you usually clean your shoes before going to a dance?" (We'd most likely in the period before been playing football in the playground) or "Barnett, don't you own a comb?"

Then, with us suitably chastised, she would explain the steps of the different dances we would be practicing and conclude with "Boys! Take your partners for the waltz"…this would be followed by more giggles from the girls' side of the room while the boys all stared at the floor in front of them and shuffled their feet, not making a move.

We could all feel our music teachers' stare burning into us and, after a few moments, when it was obvious that no one was going to move, she would march across the floor and grab her unfortunate victim by the arm (or sometimes the ear, if the 'victim' had been making comments on the side to his pals) and propel him over to the nearest girls and make him ask her for a dance. She'd then lead the couple onto the middle of the floor where they would stand red faced and highly embarrassed until the record player commence with the waltz music. With the teacher once more by their side they would attempt the waltz while the teacher counted loudly, "One, two, three, one, two, three…"

With the teacher thus distracted, the gamer of the boys would cross the dance floor and pick a partner; this was the signal for a mad scramble from the remainder of the lads to get a partner or be left with the 'wallflowers' or 'hairy Marys' as we called them (which was most unfair on reflection, given that many of us lads were no 'oil paintings' ourselves, and what was more, most of the girls were good dancers and better scholars into the bargain!).

By the time the school dance came around, we were all quite proficient on our feet, at least with some of the dances and our focus was on which girls we'd like to dance with on the night (for there was always the 'fear' that you would be declined especially if the girl had her eye on another lad and the teacher(s) didn't see the refusal). On the night, everything usually went well, we all enjoyed the dancing, the teachers were pleased with our efforts and best of all we mostly got to walk our favourite girl home!

I'm sure that the cold autumn and winter nights added to the romance of these occasions, while the parting kiss at your girls' front door made all the embarrassment of the school dance practice sessions fade into oblivion!

One advantage of the school dances was that it gave us lads greater confidence in our ability at the scouts' and guides' dances and we'd take to the floor with gusto! (Mind you, it may also have been that at these dances the lights were dim, and on occasion non-existent, and they mainly played 'rock and roll').

Rock 'n' roll had just hit Scotland in the early 50s and it seemed all the lads in the neighbourhood were into playing guitars (except for me who was struggling with a cello!) Next door to me the family had a couple of lads a few year older than me and every night they'd be practicing skiffle and rock music. They'd be taking off Tommy Steele singing the number one hit *'Singing the Blues'* or Marty Robbin's *'Knee deep in the Blues'*. I'd go to bed many a night listening to their music and wishing I could join them, but I doubt they'd have appreciated my cello playing! However I did have one consolation, my older friend Lindsey, who live across the road played a country guitar and often he'd come over and we'd practice singing the songs on the 'hit parade', which was another development of the 50s.

While a couple of my school pals had girlfriends of a sort from school, I tended to find myself drawn more to the girls I mixed with at the scouts' dances as well as girls from the orchestra and the pipe band I played in.

It was girls (and boys) from all these areas as well as cousins and friends that made up the group that came to parties at my parents place. Mum and Dad encouraged me to have parties (I think mainly because they had done the same thing with their friends in their younger days), and I would usually have one or two parties a year leading into the festive season.

Our home in Kinellar Drive was excellent for parties as it had a separate living room and dining room, so there was space to 'play' party games, (In the '50s, most families in Glasgow lived in corporation houses many of which were small and didn't have the rooms we had.)

There would be up to thirty or so of my friends at my parties and they all mixed well, with not quite a few romances emanating from such nights, which was little wonder given that most of the night was taken up with playing games such as 'postman's knock', 'cushiony', 'subways' and 'spin the bottle'…all kissing games! We also danced and listened to the latest 'pop' tunes as well as playing 'pass the parcel' and 'musical chairs' (which could also become a 'kissing' version!)

I'm unsure where these (kissing) games came from, I know from my mum that such games were popular at parties in her young days, while 'postman's knock' has always been a favourite party game for all ages where boys and girls were concerned.

However such games seem to have been 'lost' to the generations that followed on from the '60s; perhaps it was the accessibility of motor cars to teenagers and the so called 'sexual revolution' which saw the demise of such innocent fun…but we enjoyed our parties and not a few romances developed from 'boy meeting girl' over the years.

There were lots of parties and dances in our teenage years, and most of the groups I was a member of had their own celebrations throughout the year. I well remember one weekend away with the Knightswood Junior Orchestra at

Montrose House, which was an old manse used as a type of youth hostel situated at Balmaha on Loch Lomond.

We were there for a weekend of outdoor activity...but it was the indoor activity that made the weekend! After a day of walking in the hills the evening concluded with a singalong around the open fire in the main room of the manse, which in its heyday would have been the ballroom. About 10:30 pm or so we all retired to our respective dormitories...

...well for a little while at least, for once we felt confident that the adults were settled down in their rooms, the boys headed for the girls dorm where our opposite numbers were waiting to play 'subways'! (a game which starts by partnering off and 'smooching' under the blankets with the lights off, then when the boy or girl designated as the 'stationmaster' switches on the lights, partners were changed and the lights go off and once again you are in the 'subway'!)

As you can imagine, with a roomful of youngsters 'pashing on' there was quite a bit of frivolity too, along with the hugging and kissing and we were oblivious to the noise we were making with our good-humoured banter. Suddenly the door of the dorm opened and Dad's head appeared around it (Dad was in charge of the weekend.) We all shot up from under the blankets not quite knowing what to expect. Dad just looked at me with my arms still round my girl, winked and said, "O.K. Mac, time to turn in!" and his head disappeared. We all looked at each other, then with a few giggles and a parting kiss the boys trooped dutifully back to their own dormitory. But it had been a weekend to remember and was talked about for many a month after the event.

Valentine's Day (14 February) was always a big event when I was at high school, though I never gained much from it! The popular lads (or good-looking ones) would be inundated with valentines. It was not unusual for one of my pals to get upwards of a dozen cards from female admirers; me, I never got one! It was the first question asked come Valentines' Day, "How many cards did you get?"..."None!"

Those with cards would show them off during the morning break or at lunchtime, and with the help of the 'less fortunate' try to guess which girl sent which card (cards were never signed.) Not only was there valentine cards on show but there would be chalked verses scribed on the playgrounds extolling undying love for a certain boy or girl.

The only consolation about these was when spied by a teacher some unfortunate boy (girls were never humiliated!) would be told to get a bucket of water and remove the verse (or worse) immediately. This would be done to the background of jeers and laughter from those at the scene!

I wasn't the only lad (or girl for that matter) who didn't get a valentines card, but it didn't help that some got so many! I could well relate to the feelings of Charlie Brown in the comic strip *'Peanuts'* who, like me went through the frustration and disappointment year after year without getting a card – it wasn't as though we didn't have girlfriends!

I could relate too with Charlie Brown and his wanting to give the little red haired girl a valentine. In my second year of high school I had my heart set on a girl who I had danced with a couple of times at our scout dances and Christmas parties and I badly wanted to give her a card, but like Charlie Brown I just couldn't pluck up the courage!

Unlike today's valentine cards, where the verse says it all, in the '50s, there would be many rhymes handwritten in the card which sometimes gave a clue to the person who sent the card.

Some verses were cute or clever, like…

'Tulips in the garden, tulip in the park,
but there's nothing like two lips kissing after dark'

or

'A hundred years or more ago a man with powder in his gun went out to hunt a deer; but nowadays a dear with powder on her nose goes out to hunt a man.'

Of course there was always the risky one, usually scribbled on the asphalt of the playground…

'I love you, I love you, I love you almighty,
I wish your pyjamas were next to my nightie,
Don't be mistaken, don't be misled,
I mean on the clothesline, not in the bed!'

So even if some of us didn't receive cards, we could still enjoy the verses as we helped our pals try to decide which girl had sent the card!…

Of course us 'unlucky' ones could always console ourselves with the knowledge that we did have girlfriends and we seldom walked home from a dance alone...but why didn't they send us a card!

'Sex' (or 'winching' as it was called in Glasgow) in the '50s was about 'pashing on', and heavy petting was about as far as things went with the opposite sex; 'puppy love' was still soft and tender with little or no sexual overtones. It was the days of Pat Boone and Connie Francis and there was nothing better than dancing close to your girl to the slow dance called the 'mooney', to the latest ballad. The boys hold their hands against the sides of his girl's hips while she would drape her arms around her partners neck. Many a night would conclude with this dance and the voice of Connie Frances singing, 'Who's sorry now' or Pat Boone's Ain't that a shame' echoing across the dance floor.

The dance got its name through Hal Mooney who was at one time a pianist with the Jimmy Dorsey Orchestra ; his arrangements were 'slow swing'.

After the dance, if it was not too late, we'd make for our favourite milk bar to share a milkshake before the walk home. There would always be some fun as we tried to fit into the one cubicle with the girl's rope petticoats taking up all the room! Rope petticoats were all the rage with the girls along with gingham blouses with the collars stiffened and turned up, while the boys fashion statement was 'winkle picker' shoes (shoes with a long-pointed toe).

I spent a small fortune on my first pair of winkle pickers, burgundy brown alligator leather! Before a date, I would spend hours polishing them to a mirror shine!

Hairstyles were also most important and it could take a considerable time to get the coiffure above your forehead and your DA just right (the hair style at the back of the head was called a DA because it looked like a duck's arse).

But even in the '50s, it cost to take a girl on a date...whether you shared milkshakes or not. So I had to find a way to subsidise my pocket money if I was to be in the dating game. And I found this through my pal Dougie who did a paper run for the local newsagent. I first got involved through doing Dougie's run when he was sick or had other commitments, and when a run became vacant the proprietor offered me a job.

Mind you, a paper run in Glasgow in the '50s was not all 'beer and skittles'. While the pay was good (on a good week I could make three pounds – I only got five pounds a week as an apprentice when I started work in Australia in '59), the weather and early morning starts, especially in winter, could make for a trying start to the day.

Also, for a paper run, you had to have a good and reliable bike, and as Dad's 'policeman's bike' was not suitable, being an old fashioned square-framed model without gears and almost impossible to pedal uphill, I had to find a new set of wheels. I did this by buying a second-hand frame from Dougie, acquiring the necessary wheels, saddle etc., and putting it all together with a fresh coat of paint.

With the paper run secured, I then had the wherewithal to indulge in the fashions of the day as well as being able to date girls without the fear of my finances running out!

With the advent of rock 'n' roll and the influence of mid-west America, jeans had just come onto the market. I bought my first pair almost as soon as I had the money; I couldn't believe how uncomfortable they were! Made out of heavy denim, and as stiff as boards with about a four inch (12 cm) turn up at the bottom, and it took some time to acquire the swagger that went with them! But with these, a 'baby blue' iridescent silk tie and white shirt, I was ready to play the field...

I did have another rather 'shocking' incident in my teenage years to do with my appearance and it happened when my parents gave me an electric razor for my fifteenth birthday.

One evening, I was running late for my date and I noticed a bit of 'fuzz' on my chin. I went for my electric razor. Unfortunately, on plugging it into the power point, my hands must still have been wet from doing my hair, I got an electric shock that threw me across the bathroom! I didn't use my electric razor much after that!

In a previous chapter I alluded to the 'escapades' of the members of the Knightswood pipe band and country dance team while holidaying in Holland...which was just another example of the fun we had when boys and girls get together! It was from this holiday that I entered my first serious relationship.

Irene was one of the girls in the Scottish country dance team and after the Holland trip we started 'going steady'. This was in late '57 and I was just a few months, short of my fifteenth birthday.

Over the following eighteen months our relationship developed, with the distance between our homes being no disincentive, though it did mean a walk of some five miles home for me if I missed the last tramcar from Annisland Cross back to Knightswood (no readily available taxis or mobile phones in those days!).

The tram journey to home on some nights could be an adventure in itself as the last tram always had its share of drunks making their way home after a night on the town. On more than one occasion, while sitting up the front of the top deck of the car, you'd hear the Glaswegian call, "Hey Jimmy! What are you lookin' at me fur?" and like most of the sober passengers, you'd keep your eyes to the front and ignore the remark and hope that the speaker would settle down.

Mostly the comment was made to no one in general and the drunk would settle into a seat and fall asleep, however, there was always the odd one who would want to get a reaction by 'eyeballing' a fellow passenger.

I can only remember on one occasion this leading to a 'stare out' between a drunk and myself, and as he swayed back and forth on his heels I was wondering what would happen next when the conductor arrived and threatened to put us both off the tram if we didn't sit down and behave ourselves! Thank goodness for conductors!

Having Irene as my girlfriend made the band practice nights something to look forward to which made Dad wondered what had happened as up till then, I had shown little more interest in learning the pipes than what I had with the cello! Amazing what having a girlfriend can do!

Irene and I had many good times together and it was a sad parting when I left Scotland in March of '59 to start a new life in Australia.

My other 'love affair' of my early teenage years happened prior to my going steady with Irene. It came about through my chronic eczema which saw me hospitalised for a number of weeks. In hospital, I was attended to by a vivacious nurse with a ready smile and nice personality; this was Morag and I 'fell' rather heavily for her (the nurse's uniform and black stockings may also have had something to do with this!).

Morag was a few years older than me, but she obviously had a soft spot for me and encouraged our relationship with much flirting and good humour. When she was on night duty, I used to sit with her as the night desk into the wee small hours – unless the night matron paid a visit, when I would scurry back to my ward bed!

I spent three weeks in hospital before the doctors got my eczema under control and in that time Morag and I formed quite a relationship, so much so that shortly after I was discharged from hospital Morag and her girlfriend (also a nurse) came to my home for dinner. Mum and Dad were the perfect hosts, but I'm sure they wondered what their son was getting into courting an older female.

Dad thought his worst fears were confirmed when my eczema broke out again some weeks later and I had to return to hospital. He accused me of letting my eczema get out of hand so that I could keep contact with Morag.

While this was not the case (I had terrible trouble in trying to overcome the itchiness of this skin problem and sometimes the only relief I got was to scratch, which of course started the whole thing up again), I could understand Dad's frustration as he had spent countless hours trying to help me rid myself of this affliction.

Dad had tried everything to help me overcome the problem of my itchy skin, he even had me wear leather mittens at night in an attempt to prevent me scratching while asleep, but it was all to no avail.

Luckily, this second outbreak was soon brought under control (as was my 'love affair' with Morag) and I had no major problems with eczema in the future.

Girls weren't my only interest through my teenage years, though no doubt they were the major one! I enjoyed sport and while not into team sports much, I did play for the school's rugby team as well as gaining my royal lifesaving certificate through the school.

Dad introduced my brother and me to swimming and we regularly went to Whiteinch or Dumbarton baths with some pals.

Cycling was my other outlet which I did mostly with my cousin Leslie; we'd often cycle to Loch Lomond side for the day or down to Dumbarton Rock, however my main outdoor activity was climbing, something that we did every chance Dad got at weekends or on a holiday.

Dad had been a member of the Scottish mountaineering club in his younger days and (next to Mum) a day in the Scottish hills was his first love; this was something that he wanted both my brother, Alistair, and I to appreciate. So at every opportunity it was 'off to the mountains!'

Our first sojourns were in the Campsie Fells, a range of hills rising up behind Glasgow's north; small hills but with some interesting and testing climbs. They were a great place to gain confidence before 'graduating' to the mountains around Loch Lomond and beyond. The 'Campsies' as they were known, were the most easily accessible hills from Glasgow as you could get to different parts of them by tram or bus which made for an affordable day out.

While we had many rambles over these hills, it was a couple of features closer to Loch Lomond side that I remember best for their unusual if not spectacular walks.

Close to the 'Queen's View' at Stockiemuir is a fissure of rocks named 'The Whangie' which lies on the side of Aucheneden Hill. (The 'Queen's View' in itself is always worth a visit as from the hummock you get a grand view looking up to Loch Lomond with the hills of the highlands marching off to the distance.)

The 'Whangie', which is a fault in the hillside, gave us many an exciting time over the years. A ravine some three hundred feet in length and in places over thirty feet deep, it has an aurora about it which is no doubt enhanced by the folklore that it was created by the devil!

It's said that the devil (or 'Auld Nick' as he's known is Scotland) was on his way home from a night out on the town and slightly the worst of wear. When coming over Aucheneden Hill, his tail accidentally clipped the side of the hill causing it to split asunder! We were always in awe of this place growing up…

Another place of Auld Nicks' is near Killearn, not far from the 'Whangie', called 'The Devils' Pulpit'.

This unusual place is in open fields not on a hillside, and you climb down into this split in the ground, which is some twenty to thirty feet deep and about a hundred feet in length. At the bottom there is a small burn running the length of the gully, which may have had some influence in the making of the place. From the bottom, you look up at a tangle of trees and bushes which overhang the place and make it quite dark and eerie, and the major feature is an outcrop of rock which looks much like a pulpit, hence the name 'The Devils' Pulpit'– in the bowels of the earth, whose else would it be?

Mind you, we weren't always mixing with the devil on our rambles. We also explored Rob Roy's cave, on the banks of Loch Lomond, watched as the rain made the gargoyles spout with water at the "Girnin' Gates' at Westerton ('girnin' is the scots word for crying), had picnics in the Faerie Glen at Balloch and much more.

As well as climbing such well known landmarks around Glasgow such as Dumgoyne, Dumbarton Rock and Ben Lomond, we also did many of the harder climbs around Loch Lomond and the Trossachs including 'The Cobbler' and of course the highest peak in Britain, Ben Nevis.

However, it was on the Campsies in winter that I had my first experience of the 'broken spectre'. This is a phenomenon seen by climbers when they are climbing in mist and sunshine, it looks like the shadow of a person with a halo walking towards you but in fact, it is your own shadow. It is created when the sun and mist are exactly angled on each side of the climber – quite an eerie experience and one in keeping with all the tales of the devil, witches and faeries that abound in the folklore of the hills.

These were enjoyable times in the hills. There would always be something that made our walks memorable, whether it was the sighting of red deer on a hillside ahead of us or skating on frozen lochans in the winter or perhaps a swim in the cold depth of Loch Lomond after a day out.

Often we would meet one of Dad's pals on our hikes and while they stopped for a 'blether' we would be fortified with hot cocoa and chocolate biscuits which made the day all the more enjoyable. It was all part of an appreciation of the Scottish countryside which would stay with me for the rest of my life.

The one final incident of my teenage years which stays fresh in my mind to this day and it happened only a week or so before our family left Scotland for Australia.

I was playing golf with my pal Brian (Morton) and we were sharing Dad's set of golf clubs as Brian didn't have any; we weren't very skilled at the game having never played much. We were on about the third tee as I remember and Brian had just hit off, it was a terrible shot hooking hard to the left and into some trees near the boundary fence of the course.

Brian was concerned about finding his ball and took off down the left side of the fairway. I suggested he wait till I hit but he continued on his way. I hit my shot and also hooked it left, I yelled, "Fore!" which made Brian turn round and my ball hit him direct in the eye! He went down like a ton of bricks! I raced up to him to see blood pouring out of his eye and Brian in pain saying he couldn't see. I told him to hold his eye closed with his hand over it while I went for help.

As we were quite some way from the golf club, the quickest way for me to get help was to scale the boundary fence and seek assistance from one of the houses bordering the course – it took me three attempts before someone would open their door and let me call for an ambulance! When the ambulance came, Brian was taken straight to the infirmary where luckily, they were able to save his eye.

This incident really shook me up as Brian and I were good pals and had been in the scouts together. I felt so bad about what had happened that I gave Brian my (Dad's) set of golf clubs – Dad never said anything about this, but it must have been a shock to him that I gave away his set of steel-shafted golf clubs (which would have cost quite a bit in the mid '50s).

Next time I saw Brian, he had a patch over his eye which had to stay in place for some time, but he was quite 'upbeat' about the whole incident and when I left for Australia we were still the best of pals. (I was to meet up with Brian again some forty years later when he emigrated to Australia.)

Dad had starting talking about migrating to Australia or New Zealand (he tended to lean towards the latter because of the mountains) when Mum's cousin, Isa Howie, migrated to Australia in '56.

Dad would bring this concept into the conversation around the dinner table; he'd often say, "Right, who wants to go to New Zealand?" (or sometimes it was Australia). At first he didn't get much response, Alistair being the only one who showed an interest, Mum was definitely not interested and my sisters tended to watch for her reaction while I was too busy being a teenager. But Dad persisted and he would bring magazines and articles home about these countries.

Dad corresponded regularly with Aunt Isa and by '58, he'd made up his mind that the future for his family lay in the Southern Hemisphere and when because of immigration requirements and the need for a sponsor New Zealand was not viable, he set his sights on Australia. He was encouraged by Aunt Isa who often wrote saying we had to come and see Australia as we'd love it (how right she was).

By this time Aunt Isa settled in the southern seaside suburb of Sydney called Cronulla and indicated that she and her husband, George, would be willing to sponsor our family and we could stay with them in the short term, should we decide to immigrate.

Dad persisted with his dinner talk, "Hands up those wanting to go to Australia?" and one day it happened, Mum raised her hand, the girls followed suit and we were committed. In late '58, Dad got the offer of an assisted passage to Australia…

In April '59, our family set sail for Australia aboard the P&O Liner the TSS Strathaird…I was leaving a lucky childhood behind to start a great adventure twelve thousand miles away in the land known as 'The Lucky Country' – and it was for me, but that's another story…

The P&O liner S.S. Strathaird, which we sailed on to Australia.

Alastair and me with Santa 1949

Christmas 1951 with Fiona
(on my knee) Alastair & Lana

Christmas at our home in 1953 with Gran waddell.
Mum is showing Alastair how the puppet works.

Bankhead Primary School 1950s
I am 2nd from left top row

At Dunoon Pier with Mum's cousin Isa
(the lady who sponsored our family to Australia)

1954 Climbing Conic Hill behind Balmaha Alastair is showing his strength rock lifting ! My pal Dougie & I are in the background

Near the peak of Conic Hill

Looking across Loch Long to the Cobbler
which I climbed many times
in my younger years with family and friends

*1954 – Climbing the Cobbler with
my Cousin Leslie and Pal Barry*

1954 – On the Cobbler

Victoria Drive Senior Secondary School

...and all that was left when I returned in 1990!

The first exchange group 1955, from Finland on a day outing to West Kilbride. I'm sitting on the sand front row with my pal Dougie standing (middle of picture)-1955

Class of '58 - I'm top left

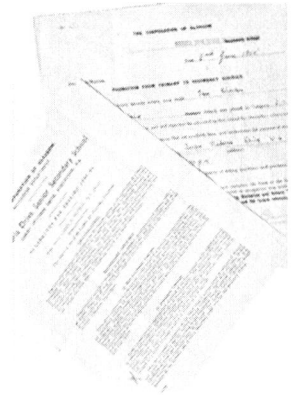

My acceptance into high school

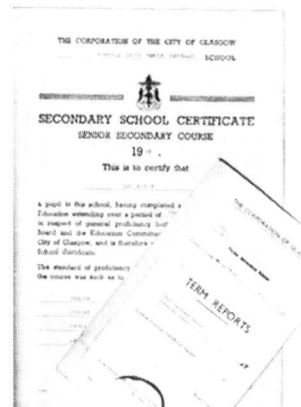

...and my secondary school certificate – thank goodness I emigrated!

*Whiteinch Baths where we swam with the
school and did our royal life saving course*

the baths were where Dad took Alastair , me and my pals each Thursday night .
The 'hot tubs' where Alastair used to hide are behind the person standing in the back of the
photo. You can see the balcony of the 2nd floor of the baths on the left from where we used to
'bomb' swimmers! We were usually caught and thrown out !

'59 last photo taken at Gran & Granpa Waddell's house before leaving for Australia. Gran &
Granpa Waddell are front right with my Gran Marshall in middle. The children are our cousins
from Dad's side of the family.

March '59 last family photo before leaving for Australia

*On Loch Lomond with my pals from the
110th scouts group; Barry, Tom & Brian*

At the top of Ben Lomond

*Scouting memorabilia - American neckie & Woggle from Jamboree, 110th Scouts magazines;
woggle neckie of Scottish contingent
and the Jamboree commemorative book mark given to all UK contingent*

Entrance to the World Scout Jamboree

*The Jubilee Journal was the newspaper
of the World Scout Jamboree*

Flag Raising started each morning

*In the 2nd week of the Jamboree
we were flooded!*

1948 on the sands at Goorock with
Mum, Dad and Alastair

Second holiday 1950 with Dad's brother
(Uncle Bruce) and his wife (Aunt Margaret) and
their daughter Elizabeth, Lana born in '49, is on Mum's knee

1951 on holiday in Arbroth. The latest addition to our family Fiona, is in the pram, Lana has learned to walk and Alastair and I are getting used to wearing kilts!

*Building sandcastles on the
shore at Arbroath 1951*

Alastair & me on the beach at Anstruther '54

Our First Exchange Holiday to Denmark in '54 We stayed with the Johansson Family at Hvidore. I played football in the local park with their two boys Torgan & Kirk

Visiting the famous statue of
'the Little Mermaid' ...again in kilts!

'55 saw us visit Italy (no lilts this time, weather was too hot!!!)
This is us in front of the Vatican

In '55 we had an exchange group from Finland. This is taken outside Knightswood community centre before we took the group on a tour of the Trossachs. Somehow I managed to get in the centre of the picture!

'56 my first flight
Off to Holland with the Knightswood Pipe Band

'57 the Danish Girls Choir outside the community centre. The choir gave performances at a number of venues in Glasgow

On holiday in '57 at Carnoustie with my Dutch friend Bob Joosten (bottom left of picture)

'57 above Dumbarton Rock overlooking the Clyde. On a day's hike with Bob Joosten

1958 our last holiday in Scotland.
On the sands of Morar on the West coast of Scotland.

Picnic on the sides of Loch Lomond '58.
This is the van that got sideswiped
by a motorbike & sidecar on us leaving the picnic area.

1958 the Knightswood Junior Orchestra. I'm on the left with my Cello.

One of the many parties held at my parent's house during my teenage years. The group is mainly from the orchestra and 110th Scout group. My cousin Leslie is at the bottom right of picture.

Taken in '59 again with my orchestra friends as well as school friends.
My cousin Elizabeth is in the middle row far left , while Leslie is bottom right with a girl on his knee.

March '59 saying 'goodbye' to
Davina & Nicki (from the Orchestra)

Addendum to 'The Last of the Lucky Childhoods' (Poetry)

Over lain's years of writing poetry, he has often reminisced in rhyme about his Scottish childhood,
Some of the poems which have a connection to his memoir are produced in the following pages.

Johnny Weiss' Mother

When my brother and me were only wee
Dad taught us how to swim
He'd take us to the whiteinch Baths
Where we learned to dive right in

And as our swimming strokes improved
Dad would say to me and my brother
You're doing fine boys, you're looking good
Just like Johnny Weiss mother

Now this seemed kind of strange to me
For I'd never heard that name
A mother who was a great swimmer
Was dad just playing games?!

So I often wondered about Johnny's mum
Whose swimming dad extolled
And wondered how could she be so good

'Cause aren't all mums old?
Then one day at the pictures show
I was watching my hero Tarzan
Then the credits rolled across the screen
It hit me – Johnny Weissmuller was a man!!!

Yesteryears & Halloween

I find my thoughts are far away
As Halloween draws near
My mind goes back to childhood days
Of Scotland…and yesteryear

October nights with frosty ground
And child excitement all around
Our group from door to door would go
With turnip lanterns all aglow
Witches ghost and faery queen
Asking "please may we have our Halloween?"

Adults at doorways in mild surprise
Exclaim "is that wee Sheila in that guise?
Inside each house we'd all perform
A song a dance or even a poem

Each child would then receive some pay
And with a thankyou be on their way
Tired but happy late that night
We'd count our takings by firelight

Walnuts apples and threepenny bits
Would all slip through our fingertips?
Then with fancy dress left strewn around
It's off to bed and sleeping sound
And dream of times that might have been
Of yesteryears and Halloween

Peas Brose

When I was wee, the food was plain,
though some had quite unusual names,
we had plain old 'tatties' wi' mince,
as well as 'veggies' that made me wince...

We had 'fish suppers' and porridge as well,
and Scotch Broth which was really swell,
but the one that really got up my nose,
was a orangey/brown paste they called 'Peas Brose'...

However I came to like 'Peas Brose' fine,
but when we left Scotland in '59.
In Australia, 'Peas Brose' was not to be found
no matter how much I looked around...

Well, I kind of missed that unusual taste,
of 'Peas Brose' made into a paste,
so back in Scotland some years later,
I thought for 'Peas Brose' they'd surely cater...

I'd breakfast on 'Peas Brose' with milk, piping hot,
but on requesting same what a surprise I got,
'Peas Brose' no shop had heard of that,
one asked , "is it something for the cat?"!

Each time I went to that land I used to call 'hame',
I searched for 'Peas Brose' but all in vain,
then a old friend said, "Och, you're living in the past,
you'll no get that fur today's breakfast!"!

(from some notes taken in Scotland)

Black Puddin' oan a Roll

In a wee café in Drymen toon
We thought we'd stap tea dine
An' when the menu came aroon,
A thoucht, this'll dae me fine

'cause the menu wis Scottish fare,
Like, black pudding oan a roll,
An' iron bru tae slake yer thirst
A thoucht a'd kicked a goal

Now , black puddin' a'd had mony a time
But never in a bun
A'd ne'er heared the like o' it before
But a thoucht it micht be fun

So a ordered up a black puddin' roll
Wi' chip oan the side
An iron bru tea tap it aff
Wi' nae thouchts fur ma inside!

But a hae tae say
It wasnae real bad
Unusual , that may be true
But nae trip tae Scotland wid be complete
Without black puddin' an iron bru!

Be kind tae yer Granny!

Be kind tae. yer Granny,
Fur she's yer Mammy's Mammy,
An'yer Mammy is the wan who luvs ye true....

So, though yer Granny's auld,
An' canna stoan the cauld,
Be kind tae her, nae metter whit ye do....

An' if yer Granny canna hear,
Jist whisper in her ear,
An' be kind tae her, nae metter whit ye do....

An' if yer Granny's feelin' weak,
Jist peck her oan her cheek,
An be kind tae her nae metter whit ye do....

An if yer Granny's a wee bit funny,
Aboot hoo she spends her money,
Be kind tae her nae metter whit ye do....

Fur jist remember rhis......
If ye didnae hae a Granny,
Ye windae hae a Mammy,
Then who the de'il would then look efter you?!!!

(Concept from old Scottish song: 'Ye canna shuv yer Granny aff a bus')

Monarchs of the Glen

The Scottish scenery is breathtaking
Its lauded far and wide
But there's something within that scenery
That most folks can't abide

The locals treat them with respect
These Monarchs of the Glen
But it's not the deer I speak here
These are much less visible than them!

They're sometimes besides the loch side,
They prefer a windless day
As they dance and jingle in the air
Awaiting their unsuspecting prey

You may not be aware of them
Because of their size
But when they bite you
They'll bring tears into your eyes!

These bitie little monsters
Midges are their name
Are known as Monarchs of the Glen
Cause that is their domain

If you're ever attacked by these wee pests
When wandering in a glen
I'll bet you a pound to a penny
You'll no go there again!

Valentine's Day

14th February – St. Valentine's Day,
a day when young lovers have their say,
and Valentine cards were all the rage,
when I was at school in my younger days…

The girls really set the scene,
Giving cards to boys on whom they were keen,
And in each card they'd write a poem,
And sign it with – name unknown!

'Rose are Red, Violets, blue,
I think I have a crush on you'

And any boy that the girls adored,
Would get Valentine cards by the score,
While the lesser lights, of which I was one,
Sometimes got a few – sometimes NONE!

But, at the Valentine's dance that night,
Not a card would be in sight,
And every boy would have a pretty 'miss'
And the night would end with a goodnight kiss......

'Tulips in the garden, Tulips in the park,
but there's nothing like Two lips,
kissing after dark'...

Brylcream

Brylcream was all the rage,
When I was just a lad,
Most of the men would wear it,
But not so my old Dad...

You'd see it advertised everywhere,
Buy it in a tube or jar,
'A little dab'll do you',
Make you feel just like a star...

There were brylcream machines everywhere,
And, for a penny in the slot,
You'd get a squirt of hair cream,
From a nozzle it was shot!

But us lads who had no money,
We found another way,
We'd suck the brylcream from the nozzle,
So we didn't have to pay!

Then we'd spit the cream onto our hands,
And run them through our hair,
Then comb it in the latest style,
And thought we looked a lair!

Now this method had a small problem,
if your were going on a date,
for the taste of brylcream on your lips ,
was a thing all girls would hate

Thoughts of Christmas Past

I gaze into the Christmas lights,
as I sit in the quietness of the night,
the hour is late on Christmas Eve,
and my mind wanders into make-believe…

And, I wonder where the years have gone,
since I was a child on Christmas morn,
awaiting for Dad to call, "Santa has been!"
and we'd all run downstairs with a scream!

We'd scramble 'round the Christmas tree,
opening presents with untold glee,
our voices would be filled with joy,
as we each discovered a favourite toy…

Once presents were opened to the window we'd go,
to see if overnight 'Santa' had brought snow,
and if the ground was covered all in white,
we'd run outside for a snowball fight!

Later, Christmas dinner and an open fire,
what more could any child desire?
later still, it's time for bed,
with pleasant dreams in a sleepy head…

The years rolled by and my children came,
and the magic of Christmas was still the same,
my daughters , wide awake on Christmas morn,
would await my call…"Santa has gone!"

They would rush downstairs with excitement in their eyes,
to see what 'Santa' left as a surprise,
but outside they didn't look for snow,
it was sunscreen on and to the surf they'd go…

Now my grandkids are the ones,
who's eyes light up when 'Santa' comes,
and as I see them filled with glee.
I remember Christmases when I was wee…

Smith's Potato Chips

Crisps, they come in all flavors now
In packets big and small
But there was only one kind of crisp
In my childhood I recall

SMITH'S CHIPS were the only crisps
When I was a wee land
They always were a special treat
Bought for us by our dad

We'd get them maybe once a week
Dad called them a chittering bite
They stopped our teeth from chattering
After swims on a wintry night

They came in bright blue packets
Not crinkle cut just plain
And they only had one flavor
Potato was its name

And they came unsalted
For there wasn't the 'know how'
To cook them with the flavor
Like they do as now

But in each and every packet
Unless there was a fault
Was a twist of blue waxed paper
Which inside contained some salt!

You'd sprinkle the salt into the bag
Then gave it a good shake
This give your chips a flavor
Of which there was no mistake

And I wonder if the kids today
Would get anything like the fun
From opening a packet of Smith's Chips
The like of which we had when we were young